2016年度西北工业大学人文社科创新基金
(编号:G2016KY0202)支持

PAIQIU YUNDONG HANYING XIAOCIDIAN
排球运动汉英小词典

主　编　王　成　杨　林

副主编　阮红梅　景　旺　王均松

西北工业大学出版社

西　安

【内容简介】 本词典是一部排球专业的汉英词典,通过语料库的方法对排球领域的词汇进行聚类统计,收录了 4 000 多词条。本词典内容紧扣当前排球运动教学、训练与竞赛的实际需要,可以为排球教练员、运动员和球迷进行国际交流,提供良好的语言服务;为排球教学训练管理的研究工作提供便利,以帮助我国排球工作者更好地了解排球基本知识,参与国际排球交流活动,消除国际排球运动语言交流的障碍。

图书在版编目(CIP)数据

排球运动汉英小词典/王成,杨林主编.—西安:
西北工业大学出版社,2018.11
ISBN 978-7-5612-6345-7

Ⅰ.①排… Ⅱ.①王… ②杨… Ⅲ.①排球运动—词典—汉、英 Ⅳ.①G842-61

中国版本图书馆 CIP 数据核字(2018)第 251937 号

策划编辑:唐小林
责任编辑:李阿盟 朱辰浩

出版发行: 西北工业大学出版社
通信地址: 西安市友谊西路 127 号 邮编:710072
电　　话: (029)88493844　88491757
网　　址: www.nwpup.com
印　刷　者: 兴平市博闻印务有限公司
开　　本: 850 mm×1 168 mm　　1/64
印　　张: 5.125
字　　数: 159 千字
版　　次: 2018 年 11 月第 1 版　2018 年 11 月第 1 次印刷
定　　价: 28.00 元

编辑委员会

主　编：王　成　杨　林
副主编：阮红梅　景　旺　王均松
成　员：(按姓氏笔画排序)

　　　　王竞秀　刘馨怡　吴静娴　张　晓
　　　　郭　琪　董　路

序

一次,与王成老师聊天时,他谈到想编写一部有关排球运动的汉英词典。他说,这会在很大程度上为参与排球活动的有关人士提供方便。这种方便不仅仅体现在进行国际交往之中,而且还十分有利于他们阅读理解国际排联的官方文件与规则。

王成老师1993年毕业后,来到西北工业大学从事体育教学工作至今,专项教学和训练的项目就是排球。中国排球事业近年来蓬勃发展,特别是中国女排在国际赛场上高歌猛进,而国内目前却还没有一部排球方面的汉英词典,王成老师越来越觉得很有必要编写一部排球领域的汉英词典,以满足排球相关人士国际交往的需要。

王成老师酷爱排球事业。他1998年晋升为国家级排球裁判。在2008年北京奥运会期间,他执裁了男子排球冠亚军决赛。因而这部词典的编写,在某种程度上是王成老师在多年排球事业中的一种有关英语语言的深切感悟。他的这种感悟感染了我们,大家一起努力完成了这部词典的编写。这部词典的出版可以消除排球领域国际交流中的障碍。

编写词典是一件非常耗时的工作,也是一项非常细致的工作。从词项的选择到释义的定夺无不渗透着编者的汗水与辛劳。这部词典从动笔到完稿用了两年多的时间。对于英文条目的汉语翻译,有的是已经被广大的排球工作者广泛接受的,有的还需要给出符合排球运动实际的汉语翻译。尽管术语翻译不需要进行句子的重组,但是为了让英语的排球术语符合汉语的表达,通俗易懂,往往是"只为一个字,捻断数根须"。这些努力及汗水换来了今天的成果,这是一件十分可喜可贺的事情。

这部词典收录了排球运动几乎所有的汉语术语,并通过计算机技术的帮助,对这些术语的使用频率进行甄别,并进行排序,这在很大程度上方便了读者的使用;而且,对于某一汉语术语,我们还给出了英语中的多个释义,便于读者挑选更容易接受的表达方式。

我们在编写过程中,努力追求英语表达的准确性。英语的表达方式也通过语料库的方法进行了检验。本词典不仅涉及排球专业的核心词汇,而且还收录了相当数量与排球运动有关的训练术语及生活用语。这在很大程度上也能够帮助从事排球运动的运动员与教练员进行赛场外的交流。

希望本部词典今后可以为广大排球教练员、运动员和球迷提供良好的语言服务,为排球教学训练管理的研究工作提供便利。

杨 林

2018 年 8 月

前　　言

体育领域的发展与社会经济的发展息息相关,排球运动在体育领域发展中起着不可或缺的作用。中国女排2004年斩获雅典奥运会冠军,2015年勇夺世界杯赛冠军,2016年里约奥运会再夺奥运冠军,她们的骄人战绩促进了我国排球运动的蓬勃发展,也加快了我国排球事业走向国际化的步伐。新的时代背景和发展机遇对排球教练员、运动员以及裁判员提出了新的国际化要求,为了适应排球项目国际化趋势与"一带一路"发展战略,本词典编委会编制了这本排球运动汉英小词典。

本词典是一部排球专业的汉英词典,通过运用语料库的方法,对排球运动领域的汉英词语进行聚类统计,收录了4 000多词条,其内容紧扣当前排球运动教学、训练与竞赛的实际需要,可以为排球教练员、运动员和球迷进行国际交流提供良好的语言服务,为排球教学训练管理的研究工作提供便利,以帮助我国排球工作者更好地了解排球基本知识,阅读理解国际排联的官方文件与规则,参与国际排球交流。

本词典主要针对国内喜爱排球运动的诸多群体,具有专业性、精练性、规范性、代表性、普及性等特点,简洁实用,检索方便,希望能成为服务于排球项目的便利工具,为排球运动的发展贡献微薄之力。

本词典由王成、景旺负责收集原文资料、统稿和校对;杨林、阮红梅、王均松负责词条分类、词义翻译和建立排球专业术语料库;王竞秀、刘馨怡、张晓、郭琪参与了词条分类、词义翻译和建立排球专业术语料库的工作;吴静娴、董路参与了收集资料、统稿和校对。

本词典在编写过程中得到了西北工业大学各级领导及相关专家的大力支持。2016年度西北工业大学人文社科创新基金(项目编号:G2016KY0202)也为本词典的出版提供了有力的项目与资金支持。同时,还要感谢所有的同仁为了本词典的出版所给予的各种鼓励与关爱,特别感谢国家体育总局排球运动管理中心蔡毅先生、天津体育学院曲正中教授、首都体育学院钟秉枢教授、中山大学李铁鸣教授、美国北德州大学张涛教授提供的帮助与指导。

尽管力求这部词典的内容准确、严谨,但由于水平有限,词典中难免有疏漏及不足之处,恳请读者批评指正。

编　者

2018 年 8 月

目　录

凡例 ································· 1

音节索引 ····························· 3

笔画索引 ····························· 11

字母索引 ····························· 28

词典正文 ····························· 29

附录 ································· 233

  附录 1　生活用语 ··············· 233

  附录 2　"鹰眼挑战"常用语 ······· 266

  附录 3　记录常用语 ············· 269

  附录 4　裁判员常用语 ··········· 276

  附录 5　教练员常用语 ··········· 288

参考文献 ····························· 310

凡　例

关于词语排序说明：

1. 同一中文词组的英语翻译，根据使用频率高低的原则进行排序。

2. 中文词组排列原则：单字条目一律按汉语拼音字母顺序排列；同音异调字按声调顺序排列（阴平、阳平、上声、去声）；同音异形字按笔画排列，笔画少的在前，多的在后；笔画相同的按起笔笔形顺序排列：横、竖、撇、点、折；第一笔笔形相同的按第二笔笔形的顺序排列，依此类推。

3. 多字条目按第一个字排列于所属单字条目之后。同一单字条目下有两个以上多字条目时，遵照上述单字排序办法按第二个字的汉语拼音顺序、音调、笔画多少及笔顺排列；第二个字相同时，按第三个字排序，依此类推。

4. 关于标点符号：双引号本身不参与排序，但其中的内容要遵照上述排序办法参与排序;括号不参与排序,并且其中的内容也不参与排序;省略号不参与排序;连接号不参与排序;顿号不参与排序;乘号按"乘"字遵照上述办法参与排序。

5. 阿拉伯数字按其对应的中文汉字遵照上述办法参与排序。

6. 以字母开头的词组(如:FIVB 标准)被编排到与其英文首字母相同的拼音组别中,在排序时将每个单个字母作为一个单字条目与中文词组进行对比排序。

7. 为方便读者查阅,本词典采用音节、笔画以及字母索引。其中,词典正文中的全中文词组可以使用音节、笔画索引进行检索,而以字母开头的词组不纳入音节、笔画的索引,仅在字母索引中进行排序。

8. 词典正文中以向右缩进两字表示上下行是一个完整的部分,而不是新的词组或释义。

音节索引

A

ai	29
an	29
ao	29

B

ba	30
bai	30
ban	30
bao	30
bei	32
ben	33
bi	33
bian	37
biao	38
bie	39
bo	39
bu	39

C

ca	42
cai	42
can	43
ce	43
cha	45
chang	45
chao	46
che	47
chen	47
cheng	47
chi	47

chong	48	ding	60
chou	49	diu	60
chu	49	dong	60
chuan	50	dou	60
chuang	52	du	60
chui	52	duan	60
ci	52	dui	61
cong	52	dun	64
cu	52	duo	64
cuo	52		

D

E

		e	66
da	53	er	66
dai	54		

F

dan	55		
dao	56	fa	68
de	56	fan	71
deng	56	fang	73
di	57	fei	76
dian	59	fen	77
diao	59	feng	77
die	60	fu	77

G

gai	79
gan	79
gang	79
gao	79
ge	80
gei	80
gen	81
geng	81
gong	81
gou	82
gu	83
gua	83
guan	83
gui	84
gun	84
guo	84

H

hai	88
hao	88
he	88
hei	89
heng	89
hong	89
hou	89
hu	91
hua	92
huai	92
huan	92
huang	93
hui	93
hun	94
huo	94

J

ji	96
jia	101
jian	103
jiang	104
jiao	104
jie	106
jin	110

jing	113		lan	125
jiu	114		lao	128
ju	115		lei	128
jue	116		leng	128
			li	128
K			lian	129
kai	117		liang	130
kan	117		lin	131
kang	117		ling	131
kao	118		liu	132
ke	118		lu	132
kong	118		luan	132
kou	119		lun	132
kua	122		luo	133
kuai	122			
kuan	124		**M**	
kun	124		ma	134
kuo	124		man	134
			mao	134
L			mei	134
la	125		men	135
lai	125		meng	135

mi	135	pang	140
mian	135	pao	140
miao	135	pei	140
min	135	peng	141
ming	136	pi	141
mo	136	pian	141
mu	136	piao	141
		pin	142
N		ping	142
na	137	pu	143
nai	137		
nan	137	**Q**	
nao	137	qi	144
nei	137	qian	144
neng	137	qiang	147
nian	138	qiao	147
niao	138	qie	147
nu	138	qin	147
		qing	148
P		qiu	149
pai	139	qu	151
pan	139	quan	153

que	154	sheng	164
qun	154	shi	165
R		shou	168
		shu	170
rao	155	shuai	170
re	155	shuang	170
ren	155	shun	172
reng	155	si	172
ri	155	song	174
rou	156	su	174
ru	156	sui	175
ruan	156	sun	175
ruo	156	suo	175
S		**T**	
sai	157	ta	176
san	158	tan	176
sha	159	tang	176
shang	160	tao	176
shao	161	te	177
she	162	teng	177
shen	162	ti	177

tian	179	xian	194
tiao	179	xiang	194
ting	181	xiao	196
tong	181	xie	197
tou	182	xin	198
tu	182	xing	199
tuan	183	xiong	199
tui	183	xiu	199
tuo	184	xu	199
W		xuan	200
		xue	200
wai	186	xun	200
wan	186	**Y**	
wang	187		
wei	188	ya	203
wen	190	yan	203
wo	190	yang	204
wu	190	yao	205
X		ye	205
		yi	205
xi	193	yin	209
xia	193	ying	209

yong	210	zheng	219
you	210	zhi	220
yu	212	zhong	222
yuan	213	zhou	224
yue	213	zhu	225
yun	214	zhua	227

Z

		zhuan	227
		zhuang	228
zai	216	zhui	228
zan	216	zhun	228
zao	216	zhuo	229
ze	216	zi	229
zeng	216	zong	230
zhan	216	zou	230
zhang	218	zu	231
zhao	218	zui	231
zhe	218	zun	231
zhen	219	zuo	232

笔画索引

一画

一　　205

二画

八　　30
二　　66
力　　128
人　　155
入　　156
十　　166

三画

大　　53
飞　　76
干　　79

个　　80
工　　81
弓　　81
及　　98
马　　134
门　　135
千　　144
三　　158
上　　160
士　　167
卫　　189
下　　193
小　　196
已　　208
义　　208
与　　212

丈	218	切	147
		区	151
四画		日	155
贝	32	手	168
比	33	双	170
不	39	天	179
长	45	王	187
从	52	为	189
斗	60	无	191
队	61	五	192
反	72	心	198
方	73	以	208
分	77	引	209
公	81	友	210
勾	82	允	214
互	92	支	220
计	99	中	222
开	117	专	227
六	132		
木	136	**五画**	
内	137	半	30
气	144	包	30

本	33	平	142
必	36	扑	143
边	37	扔	155
出	49	申	162
处	49	失	165
打	53	示	167
代	54	世	167
电	59	甩	170
对	63	司	172
发	68	四	173
犯	73	头	182
号	88	外	186
击	96	未	189
记	100	训	201
加	101	业	205
甲	102	仪	208
节	108	议	208
纠	114	用	210
立	129	右	211
另	132	召	218
目	136	正	219
皮	141	主	225

左	232	共	82
六画		观	83
		关	83
安	29	轨	84
闭	36	过	86
场	45	好	88
成	47	合	88
冲	48	红	89
传	51	后	89
创	52	划	92
次	52	回	94
灯	56	机	96
地	57	肌	97
吊	59	纪	100
丢	60	夹	102
动	60	尖	103
多	64	讲	104
帆	71	交	104
防	73	决	116
访	75	扛	117
负	77	扣	119
各	80	扩	124

笔画索引

肋	128	休	199
米	135	血	200
名	136	压	203
年	138	亚	203
曲	152	延	203
权	153	仰	204
全	153	因	209
任	155	优	210
杀	159	有	210
设	162	再	216
收	168	在	216
死	172	阵	219
同	182	争	219
团	183	执	220
托	184	仲	224
网	187	自	229
伪	189		
先	194	**七画**	
向	194	报	31
协	197	别	39
兴	199	补	39
行	199	步	41

财	42	进	110
沉	47	近	112
赤	48	局	115
初	49	拒	115
串	52	角	116
吹	52	抗	117
低	57	快	122
抖	60	困	124
泛	73	来	125
妨	75	冷	128
附	78	利	129
改	79	连	129
杠	79	两	130
更	81	灵	131
攻	81	抢	132
护	92	没	134
还	92	每	134
极	98	尿	138
技	100	努	138
坚	103	判	139
间	103	抛	140
角	105	批	141

评	143	严	204
启	144	医	208
弃	144	应	209
抢	147	远	213
求	149	运	214
驱	152	张	218
韧	155	折	218
沙	159	肘	225
伸	162	助	226
身	162	抓	227
声	164	状	228
时	166	纵	230
识	166	走	230
体	178	足	231
条	180	阻	231
投	182	作	232
完	186	坐	232
违	188		
尾	189	**八画**	
位	189		
我	190	杯	32
系	193	变	38
		表	39

参	43	和	89
侧	43	呼	91
衬	47	弧	91
抽	49	季	101
垂	52	肩	103
单	55	降	104
到	56	径	113
底	57	净	113
典	59	沮	115
定	60	空	118
法	71	拉	125
放	75	拦	125
非	76	练	130
肺	77	录	132
供	82	轮	133
股	83	命	136
官	83	抹	136
贯	83	青	148
规	84	屈	152
诡	84	取	152
国	84	软	156
果	86	实	166

使	167	知	220
始	167	直	220
试	167	制	222
视	167	终	224
受	169	周	224
松	174	注	227
拖	184	转	227
玩	187	组	231

九画

往	188		
委	189		
卧	190	保	31
物	192	背	32
现	194	标	38
线	194	测	44
限	194	持	47
性	199	重	48
学	200	穿	50
伴	204	带	55
英	209	垫	59
鱼	212	度	60
责	216	封	77
侦	219	复	78

钢	79	迷	135
给	80	面	135
骨	83	秒	135
故	83	耐	137
挂	83	屏	143
冠	84	前	145
挥	93	侵	147
恢	93	轻	148
活	94	绕	155
急	98	柔	156
挤	99	神	164
将	104	胜	164
绞	105	施	166
结	108	拾	167
界	109	适	167
胫	113	室	168
举	115	首	169
看	117	顺	172
客	118	挑	179
临	131	挺	181
冒	134	统	182
美	134	突	182

退	184	**十画**	
弯	186		
畏	190	爱	29
屋	190	被	33
相	194	部	41
削	196	乘	47
信	199	倒	56
宣	200	俯	77
选	200	赶	79
哑	203	高	79
钥	205	海	88
诱	212	核	89
战	216	候	91
指	222	壶	91
重	224	换	92
洲	225	晃	93
轴	225	获	94
柱	227	积	97
追	228	疾	98
姿	229	捡	103
总	230	健	103
		较	106

借	110	缺	154
竞	113	热	155
酒	114	弱	156
俱	116	哨	162
课	118	射	162
宽	124	素	174
捞	128	速	174
离	128	损	175
挛	132	特	177
拿	137	调	180
难	137	通	181
脑	137	挽	187
能	137	涡	190
旁	140	夏	194
配	140	效	197
疲	141	胸	199
瓶	143	验	204
起	144	娱	212
悄	147	预	212
窍	147	原	213
请	149	圆	213
拳	154	造	216

展	216		假	102
站	217		检	103
真	219		渐	104
秩	222		矫	105
准	228		脚	106
捉	229		教	106
资	229		接	106
			颈	113
十一画			救	114
			距	116
常	45		控	118
粗	52		累	128
得	56		领	132
第	58		猛	135
符	77		密	135
辅	77		敏	135
副	78		排	139
盖	79		盘	139
够	83		捧	141
毫	88		清	149
黄	93		情	149
混	94		球	149
基	97			

躯	152	章	218
蛇	162	职	222
深	164	掷	222
绳	164	综	230
授	169	做	232
随	175		
弹	176	**十二画**	
探	176	奥	29
淘	176	编	38
梯	177	裁	42
停	181	策	44
推	183	插	45
脱	184	敞	46
晚	187	超	46
象	196	朝	47
斜	197	程	47
虚	199	登	56
旋	200	等	56
掩	204	短	60
移	208	隔	80
隐	209	腘	86
跃	213	黑	89

滑	92	游	210
缓	92	越	213
集	98	暂	216
联	130	掌	218
量	131	装	228
落	133	最	231
牌	139		
跑	140		
骗	141		

十三画

强	147	摆	30
确	154	搬	30
稍	161	触	50
湿	166	错	52
锁	175	辐	77
提	178	腹	78
替	179	跟	81
腕	187	跪	84
喂	190	滚	84
温	190	鉴	104
握	190	解	109
循	200	锦	110
硬	210	禁	113
		跨	122

路	132	竭	109
碰	141	精	113
频	142	静	114
签	144	慢	134
群	154	漂	142
输	170	墙	147
数	170	赛	157
腾	177	稳	190
跳	180	需	199
腿	183	遮	218
微	188		
携	198	**十五画**	
新	199	暴	31
腰	205	播	39
意	209	撤	47
障	218	蝶	60
照	218	额	66
		横	89
十四画		踝	92
		箭	104
端	60	靠	118
裹	86	劈	141
截	109		

飘	141	整	219
踏	176	踵	224
躺	176		
踢	178	**十七画**	
膝	193	臂	36
鞋	198	擦	42
颜	204	瞬	172
毅	209	赢	209
影	209		
增	216	**十八画**	
镇	219	鞭	38
撞	228	翻	71
遵	231	鹰	209
十六画		**十九画**	
避	36	爆	31
薄	39	蹬	56
激	98	蹲	64
器	144	警	113
邀	205	髋	124

字母索引

F	FIVB 标准	68
	FIVB 特许	68
I	IR 制服	95
J	J 型传球	96
M	"M"阵型	134
R	RICE 法	155
U	"U"接发球阵型,"U"阵型	185
W	"W"接发球阵型,"W"式进攻队形	186
	"W"阵型	186

爱好者	fan
安全的拦网	safe block
奥林匹克的	Olympic
奥林匹克冠军	Olympic champion
奥林匹克运动	Olympic Movement
奥林匹克运动项目	Olympic sport(s)
奥委会	Olympic Committee
奥运会	Olympic Game(s)
奥运会比赛	Olympic competition
	Olympic tournament
奥运会发展演变	Olympic evolution
奥运会誓言	Olympic oath
奥运会宪章	Olympic charter

八秒之内	within 8 seconds
摆	swing
	waver
摆臂	arm swing
摆动	swing
摆弄球	dribbling
搬,带	carry
半	half
半蹲	half squat
	parallel squat
半跪垫	half-kneeling dig
半滚	half roll
半决赛	semi-final(s)
	semi-final match
半快球	semi-quick
	two-set
半月形防守	half-moon defense
包围圈防守	encirclement defense
包扎技术	wrapping techniques

保持	keep
保持低重心	keep low
保攻	attack after covering
保攻系统	attack coverage system
保护	cover
	cover the hitter
	coverage
保护队员	covering player
保护扣球	covering the smash
保护拦网	stop cover
保护位置	cover point
	covering position
保护一角度(一条线)	cover an angle
保护战术	covering tactics
保留	remain
报名	entry
报名表	entry form
报名单	nominal entry
报名费	entry fee
报数	count off
暴露意图	telegraph
爆发力	power

杯	cup
杯赛	cup
贝格尔表	Berger Table
背	back
背传	back pass
	back set
	back toss
	back volley
背传球	back pass
	back set
	back volley
	back toss
背垫	backward pass
背对背	back to back
背飞	back slide
	back slide attack
	backward flight
背后的战术	back set
背快	quick/C
	quick C
	quick spike from backward set
	quick spike with back set

背快球	quick-C
背溜	five set
	quick/D
	quick D
	quick-D
	quick spike from backward short set
被击的球	ball hit
被拦的扣球	blocked spike
被判罚的队员	penalized player
被驱逐的替换	substitution for expulsion
被取消资格的队员	disqualified player
被替换队员	substituted player
被允许的替换	permitted substitution
被直接拦网得分的球	stuff block
被阻拦的进攻	blocked attack
本方场区	own court
比分	score
比较	compare
比赛	competition
	game
	match

	play
比赛参加者	participants
比赛场地	playing court
比赛场地的地面	playing surface
比赛场区	playing area
比赛程序	tournament program
比赛持续时间	match duration
比赛的	competitive
比赛的裁判员	match official
比赛的基本技术	basic skills of the game
比赛的评价	match evaluation
比赛的组织	structure of play
比赛地点	competition site
比赛队伍	playing team
比赛服	uniform
比赛概念	mental conception of game
比赛馆	competition hall
比赛规则	rules of the game
比赛记录	game record
比赛间断	game interruption
	match interruption
比赛节奏	rhythm of the game

比赛结果	game results
	result of the match
比赛结果是 3∶1	the result is 3 to 1
比赛结束	end of the game
	end of match
	end of the match
比赛进行(中)	ball in play
比赛控制区域	competition control area
比赛期	competition period
比赛弃权	forfeit match
比赛情况	game situation
	playing situation
比赛日程	competition program
比赛日程表	competition schedule
比赛设施	game equipment
比赛势态	game momentum
比赛条例仪式	game protocol
比赛行动	play action
比赛意识	competitive conception
比赛战术	game tactic
比赛阵容	game line up
比赛阵势	playing pattern

比赛阵型	playing formation
比赛制	competition system
比赛制式	playing system
比赛秩序册	game schedule
比赛中的犯规	game foul
比赛中的一局	set
比赛中动脑子	play-by thought
比赛中断	ball out of play
	interruption of match
比赛中断(死球)	interruption of the rally
比赛中犯规	playing foul
比赛状态	state of play
比强力扣杀更快一些的扣球	slam spike
必须	must
闭幕式	closing ceremony
避开拦网	pass the block
	split the block
避开拦网扣直线	straight clear the block hit
避开拦网手扣球	clear the block spike
	spike past the block
臂长	arm's length

臂伸直	arm stretching
边跟进防守	side follow-in defense
	side-cover defense
	middle-back defense
	center back defense
边跟进防守体系	side-cover defensive system
	center back defensive system
边后卫	fullback
边拦网队员	end blocker
	side blocker
边上的扣球队员	outside spiker
边上的拦网队员	end blocker
	outside blocker
边线	boundary
	boundary lines
	sideline
	side line
边线裁判	linesmen
边线近网的位置	wing position
边线行为	sideline behavior
"边一二"的"W"接发球阵型	W and on wing setter

"边一二"进攻阵型	setter-in-FR formation side-pass offense
"边一二"阵型	setter-in-FR formation side-pass
边缘视觉	peripheral vision
编号	numbering
鞭	whip
鞭打	beat
	whip
鞭打动作	whiplash movement
变化	variation
标志	badge
	emblem
	mark
标志带	marker
	side bands
	sidebands
	side marker
	vertical tapes
标志带外	out of marker

标志杆	antenna
	net aerial
	vertical rod
标志线	vertical line
标准	standards
标准球	official ball
标准设备	standard equipment
表	watch
表格	sheet
表面	surface
表现	performance
别手扣球	off-hand spike
播音员	scorer
薄弱	weak
补偿训练	compensation training
补位	cover
	coverage
	seam protection
补位队员	seam protector
不带旋转的飘球	floater

不得拖延	without delay
不动脑子	no-head
不合法触球	illegal contact
不合法发球	illegal serve
不合法击球	illegal hit
不合法扣球	illegal spike
不合法请求	improper requests
不合法替换	illegal substitution
不拦网	down block
不拦网的前排队员	off-blocker
不良行为	misconduct
不良行为的判罚	misconduct penalty
不良行为等级	misconduct scale
不轮转的比赛方法	non-rotation
不能	can't
不抛起的发球	statue of liberty service
不同部位	various parts
不同的	different
	various
不要	don't

不准确的协调性	inaccurate coordination
步法	foot work
步幅	step
	stride
步子,步骤	step
部署	deployment
部署进攻	set up

擦网球	net serve
财务委员会	finance commission
裁决	deciding
裁判	referee
	umpire
裁判的判定	referee's decision
裁判的判断	referee's judgement
裁判的哨声	referee's whistle
裁判工作	refereeing
裁判人员	officiating mechanics
裁判任命书,裁判任命通知	referee's nomination
裁判实习	referee's clinic
裁判台	referee's stand
	referee's platform
裁判团	officiating team
裁判委员会	board of referees
	officiating commission
	refereeing commission

裁判员	judge
	official
	referee(s)
裁判员签字	referee's signature
裁判员用牌(红黄牌)	referee's card
裁判员暂停	official's time-out
	official's time out
裁判员正式手势	official's signal(s)
裁判长	chief referee
裁判组	refereeing corps
参加	enter
	join
侧步	side step
侧传	lateral volley
	side set
	side way(s) volley
侧传球	side volley
	side set
	lateral volley
	lateral set
侧垫	lateral pass
侧滚	side roll

侧滚垫球	rolling dig to the side
侧交叉步	two cross step
侧跨步	side step
侧跨步助跑	side step approach
侧面接球	flank receive
侧面上手发球	side overhand service
	side overhand serve
侧面下手发球	side underhand service
	side underhand serve
侧手发球	sidearm serve
	sidehand serve
侧向移动	lateral movement
侧旋	sidespin
侧旋发球	side spin service
侧旋球	side spin
侧移动	lateral movement
侧鱼跃	lateral dive
	side-dive
	side dive
测验	test
策略	tactics
	strategy

策略的	tactical
策应	support
策应防守队员	defensive coverage
策应接球队员	backing up the passer
插蜡球	ceiling serve
	lobbing service
	sky serve
插上	penetrate
	penetration
插上犯规	penetration foul
长传	long set
长凳练习	bench work
长度	length
长距离慢跑	long slow distance
长跑	distance running
长线扣球	long shot
长线球	deep shot
长远	long
常见错误	common fault
场地	court
	venue
场地尺寸	court dimensions

场地的标记	court marking
场地宽度	court width
场地侵犯	court invasion
场地四周围墙	podium
场地中央	center of the court
场点	match point
场区	court
场上队员	player on the court
场上队长	game captain
场上位置	game position
场外区域	out of bounds area
场外物体	outside object
敞开	opening
超过	outstrip
	overtake
超过次数	overtimes
(重心)超前	advance
超手扣球	smash over the block
	spike over the block
	surpass the block hit
	super-hand spike
超越	pass

朝鲜杯	Korean Cup
撤后防守	"man back" defense
撤离	release
撤手	drop hands
撤退,撤下	withdraw
沉着	aplomb
	calm
	coolness
	sangfroid
	steady
衬衣	shirt
成功率把握极高的进攻,对方无法防守	terminal attack
成绩	performance
	result
成绩记录表	chart
成员	member
乘机进攻	make the breaks
程度	degree
持	catching
	hold
持久力	staying power

持球	catch
	catching
	held ball
	hold
	holding
	lift
	throw
赤足	barefoot
冲	thrust
冲刺	dash
冲刺跑	blast
	sprint
冲上网	rush-up
冲跳	rushing take-off
	rushing take off
	rushing jump
	rushing up
重打	replay
重叠	stack
重叠拦网	tandem block
	overlapping block
重复	repeat

重复训练	reiterating training
	repeated training
	repetitious training
重赛	replay
重新	again
重新比赛	replay
重新发球	reserve
重新开始	restart
	resume
重新开始比赛	replay
重新指定	re-designation
重做	repeat
	restart
抽签	draw
	draw of lots
	drawing of lots
	toss
出场	march out
出界	out of bounds
初步报名	preliminary entry
初级的	junior
处罚	penalize

处理自由球	handling free balls
触	contact
	touch
触及	touch
触及对方场区	contact with the opponent's court
触拦网手	touch the blocker
触摸标志杆	touch the antenna
触球	ball contact
触球次数	number of contacts
触球犯规	foul in contacting the ball
触手出界	ball touched
	touch out
触手球	ball touched
触网	contact with net
	net-fault
	touch net
	touch the net
触网球	ball touches the net
穿插跑动	swing
穿过	through
穿越	penetration

穿越犯规	penetration foul
	space penetration
传低球	low set
	low ball
传递	hand
	pass
传高球	high ball
	high set
传集中球	close set
	inside set
传近网球	near-net set
传快球	quick pass
传拉开球	open set
	outside set
	wide set
传球	bump
	set
	pass
传球错位	off-hand
传球到位	on-hand
传球技术	pass work
传球角度	pass angle

传球直接过网	overset
传远网球	deep set
	far-net set
串联训练法	combination training system
串平	double attack with short low set
创伤	injury
吹哨	whistle
垂网助跑	straight approach
垂直的	vertical
次数	time(s)
次序	order
从场地两边向中间移动	outside-in
从容	take it easy
从网上反弹	bounce off the net
从网上反弹起	rebound on the net
粗鲁行为	rude conduct
错误	error
	mistake
错误的边缘	margin of error

打	play
打败	defeat
打得很松散	play loosely
打对角	opposite
打防练习	knock toss
打过	play over
打拦网手	hit off a blocker's hand
打拦网手扣球	spike off the block
打球	play ball
打手出界	wiping or tooling the block
	spike off the block
	touch-out spike
大臂	upper arm
大力发球	drive serve
	hard serve
	power serve
大力击球	hard ball
	hard drive
大力扣球	hard spike

	hard-drive spike
	power spike
	strong spike
大力抡臂	round house
大抡臂发球	round house serve
大抡臂扣球	windmill attack
大强度训练	exacting practice
	intensive training
	strenuous practice
大赛前比赛	pre-season competition
大赛前的联赛	pre-season tournament
大踏步	stride
大厅	hall
大腿,股	thigh
大斜线扣球	inside the block
	clear slash spike
大学生运动会	universiad
	University Games
大运动量训练	hard training
大重量训练	heavy weight training
代表	delegate
代表大会	congress

代表团	delegation
代表团长	head of delegation
代替	replace
带假动作的轻扣球	feint and drop spike
单脚背飞	backward flight with single foot
单脚起跳	one-footed take off
	takeoff from one foot
单人进攻	shot
单人拦网	block solo
	one-man block
	single block
单手传球	one-hand pass
	one-hand set
	single-hand set
单手垫球	one-arm pass
单手二传	single-hand toss
单手发球	one hand serve
单手红＋黄	Red＋Yellow jointly
单手抛球	one hand toss
单手前扑救球	pancake
单手调整传球	knuckler
	open-handed tip

	tip
单淘汰	single elimination system
单循环	single round-robin system
单一	single
单元,单位	unit
倒地	sprawl
倒地传球	fall down pass
	setting while falling
到达	reach
得到	get
得发球权	win the serve
得分	points
灯光	lighting
登记	register
	registration
蹬地	thrust against the ground
蹬地角度	angle of leg thrust
蹬地腿	driving leg
蹬伸	thrust
蹬腿	drive leg
等动拉力器	Mini-Gyms
等动练习	isokinetic exercises

等级	classification
等级运动员	ranking player
等张练习	isotonic exercises
低	low
低传快攻	low set and quick attack
低二传	low set
低球	low ball
	under ball
低球快攻	low set and quick attack
低手发球	underhand serve
低速进攻	off-speed attack
低姿	low-body position
	low form
	low position
低姿侧垫	low lateral pass
低姿防守	crouch defense
底角	back corner
底线	end line
底线球	deep shot
	long shot
地板	floor
地点	venue

地面	surface
地区面积	area
第二	second
第二裁判	second referee
第二裁判员	second referee
	umpire
第二次试图	second attempt
第二次暂停	second time-out
第二局比赛	second game of the match
第三次触球	third contact
第三次暂停	third time-out
	third time out
第三方场地	neutral site
第一	first
第一裁判,第一裁判员	first referee
第一场比赛	first match
第一传	first pass
第一次触球	first contact
第一次击球	first hit
第一次暂停	first time out
第一回合进攻	first round attack
第一流	first class

典礼	ceremony
电子示分牌	electronic scoreboard
垫	dig
垫步	skip
垫步跑	skipping
垫传	dig pass
垫击球	bump pass
垫球	dig
	digpass
	underhand pass
	under toss
垫球给某人扣	set sb. up for a shot
垫球失误	ball handling error
吊球	dink
	dink spike
	dinking
	drop
	drop spike
	dump
	tipp
	tipping
	soft smash with fingers

蝶坐拉伸	butterfly stretch
定名次比赛	classification league
定位防守	static defense
	stationary defense
丢发球权	loss of service
动脑筋	brain work
动态平衡能力	dynamic balance
动作	action
	movement
动作模式	action pattern
动作自如	ease
抖腕	wrist snap
斗志	fight
	fighting spirit
度数	degree
端线	endline
	end line
短	short
短传	short set
短传快攻	short set and quick attack
短吊	drop shot
短距离移动的步伐	shuffle

短裤	shorts
短跑	dash
短平错位	shift with short low set
短平快	spike with short low set
	quick/B
	quick B
	three-set
	parallel-short-toss quick spike
	quick spike from flat short set
短平快扣球	parallel-short-toss quick spike
短平快球	quick-B
短平快掩护扣球	double B
短球	short
队	team
队的表现	team performance
队的动作	team movements
队的犯规	team foul
队的击球	team hit
队的名次	teams standing
队的评估	team evaluation
队的阵容	team line-up
队的阵型	team formation

	team patterns
队服	team uniform
队形	line up
队友	teammate
队员	player
队员比赛服装	player's uniform
队员臂长	player's reach
队员触网	net touched by player-served
队员的表现	player's performance
队员的轮转	rotation of players
队员的轮转次序	player's rotation
队员的位置关系	relative position of players
队员的专业素质	specialization
队员的转队	transfer of players
队员的装备	player's equipment
队员接触球前的准备动作	ready position
队员身高	player's height
队员替换	player substitution
队员位置	player's position
队长	captain
	team captain

队长标志	identity of captain
	badge of captain
队长的签字	captain's signature
队长的请求	captain's request
对不良行为的警告	misconduct warning
对不良行为的制裁	misconduct penalty
对方	opponent(s)
	opposition
对方场区	opponent's court
对方队	opponent team
对方队员	opponent(s)
对方教练	opposing coaches
对方区域	opponent's court
对方弱点	weaknesses of opponent
对话测试	talk test
对角	opposite corner
对角线	diagonal
对角线运动	diagonal motion
对抗	compete
	opposition
对抗的	competitive
对抗练习	competitive exercise

对抗赛	dual match
对墙发球	wall serve
对球网犯规	net foul
对手	opponent
对手击球手	opposite hitter
对象	object
对照	compare
对准	align
对准球	alignment with the ball
蹲	crouch
	squat
蹲起	squats
蹲起(负重练习)	stand up from squatting position
蹲跳	knee-hop
	squat jumps
蹲跳练习	jump and skip
蹲姿	crouched position
	squatting position
蹲走	duck walk
	low walk
多次触球	multiple contacts

多点进攻	multiple-attack
多球训练法	multiple balls system
多人防守	multiple offense
多人进攻	multiple attack
多人拦网	multiple block
多组训练法	multiple sets system

额外的	extra
二传	pass
	second pass
	set
	set pass
	toss
二传插上	penetration of the setter
	running-up setter
二传换位	setter switch
二传进攻	setter attack
二传失误	toss miss
二传手,二传队员	setter
	tosser
二次进攻	dump
二次拦网	two-time block
二次球进攻	second hit attack
	second time attack
二号位	right forward
二号位队员	right forward

二人组合	two-player formation
二头肌弯曲运动	biceps curls
"二一三"防守系统	2-1-3 defensive system
"二一三"双人拦网防守阵型	two-one-three back-line cover system

F

FIVB 标准	FIVB standards
FIVB 特许	unless by agreement of FIVB
发保险球	safe service
发变化球	freak service
	varying service
发擦网球	net serve
发出	release
发高球	ceiling serve
	lobbing service
	sky serve
发飘球(一般球)	floating service
	slid serve
发球	serve
	service
发球擦网	service touching the net
发球策略	serving strategies
发球次序	order of service
	serving order
发球次序错误	error in the service order

	serving out of order
发球错误	service mistake
发球得分	serve an ace
发球的击球	service hit
发球的条件	conditions of service
发球动作	service action
发球队	team to serve
	serving team
发球队员	server
	serving player
发球犯规	service foul
	serving foul
发球方式	serving styles
发球技巧	serving techniques
发球脚故障	service foot-fault
发球练习	serving drills
发球没有过网	ball fails to pass to the opponent through crossing space
发球能手	service specialist
	serving specialist
发球区	service area
	service zone

发球区的角落	service corner
发球区线	service lines
发球区域	service area
发球权	right of serve
发球失误	loss of the service
	service error
发球时脚的犯规	crossing space fouls
	the server touches the court
	the server touches the end line
发球时球未抛起	ball not tossed or released at the service hit
发球时位置错误	out of position at service
发球试图	service attempt
发球线	service line
发球选择	service choices
发球延误	delay in service
发球掩护	blocking fault or screening
	screening
	screen during service
发球一刻队员不在场区之内	the player steps outside his/her court at the moment of the service hit
发球战术	service tactics

	serving tactics
发球直接得分	a service ace
	service ace
发球秩序	service order
发上旋球	topspin serve
发送者	sender
发跳飘球的方法	approach for jump floater serve
发下沉球	drop service
发下坠球	drop service
	sink serve
发向	serve to
发旋转球	spin serve
	spin service
发展	development
发展身体素质练习	conditioning exercise
法律根据	by laws
帆布带	canvas
	canvas band
翻滚救球	collapse
	extension roll
翻译	interpreter
翻转	tipping

反	back
反"边一二"插上	penetration of the setter
	running setter formation
	setter-in-FL formation
反"边一二"阵型	setter-in-FL formation
反弓	drawn bow
反攻	attack after defense
	counter attack
	counter offensive
反攻扣球	counter spike
反攻扣手	counter attacker
反击	counter offensive
反射	reflex
反手薄弱的区域	weak area
反手传球	backhand pass
反手发球	backhand serve
反弹	bounce
	rebound
反弹球	rebound ball
反应	reaction
	reflex
反应迟钝	slow response

反应迟缓	delay of response
反应练习	mirror drill
	reaction drill
反应能力	reaction ability
反应时	reaction time
反应速度	reaction speed
犯规	against rule
	commit a foul
	foul
犯规的	illegal
犯规的处理	consequence of a foul
犯规队	team at foul
犯规队员	player at foul
泛美运动会	Pan American Game
方法	method
方向	direction
防反	attack after defense
	serve to defend
防区	defensive area
防区的划分	division of court area
防守	defense
防守保证	defensive pledge

防守薄弱区域	weak area
防守打法	defensive play
防守的	defensive
防守的保护	defensive coverage
防守点	cover point
防守动作	defensive action
防守队	defending team
防守队员	defensive player
防守队员触及	contact by a defensive player
防守队员利用良好的站位以及手型防起对方重扣,给同伴创造反攻机会	on help
防守队员特定区域	specific territory for defenders
防守和攻防转换	defending and transitioning
防守技术	defence skills
防守空当	unprotected area
防守快速进攻	defense against quick hitter
防守拦网	defensive block
防守面积	floor coverage
防守能手	defensive specialist
防守区域	defensive area

防守趋势	defense trends
防守失误	defense errors
防守受限	defense limitations
防守体系	defensive system
防守位置	defensive position
防守系统	defensive system(s)
防守行动	defensive action
防守训练	defensive drills
防守一方	defensive side
防守移动	defensive moves
防守战略	defensive strategy
防守战术	defensive tactics
防守阵式	defensive pattern
防守阵型	defensive formation
	defensive pattern
	defensive system
防守姿势	defensive posture
防线	defensive line
妨碍	interfere
访问比赛	out match
放开	have free hands
	let go

fang

放球的架子	ball stand
放松	ease
	ease off
	ease up
	relax
	relaxation
	take it easy
放松点,别紧张	take it easy
放松法促通技术	contract-relax PNF
放松级别	relaxation class
放松跑	easy running
放松日	easy day
飞	fly
飞(位置差)	quick slide
飞行	fly
	flight
飞行轨迹	flight path
非二传手的传球技巧	setting technique for nonsetter
非法的	illegal
非受迫性失误	unforced error
非体育道德行为	unsportsmanlike conduct
非正常换人	abnormal substitution

肺系统（心肺肌）	cardiorespiratory system
分	point
分级联赛	classification league
分脚跳	straddle hop
分解动作	decomposed movement
分局点	set point
分类	classify
分散	distract
分组联赛制	tournament league system
封闭型任务	closed task
封网	seal the net
封准球	alignment with the ball
辐射状保护	radio coverage
俯卧	lie face downward
	lying face down
俯卧撑	push-up(s)
符合规则的	legal
辅助动作	supportive movements
负	loss
负场	match lost
负局	set lost
负责	be in charge of

	responsible
负重	weight leading
负重练习	stand up from sguatting position
	weight training
负重提踵练习	jumping on toes with bar on neck
	toe press
负重训练	weight training
附加赛	extra match
复杂任务	complex tasks
复杂运动的准备	preparation of movements
副裁	umpire
副裁判	umpire
副二传	co-setter(s)
	diagonal
副二传手	second setter
副攻手	co-spiker
	quick hitter
腹	abdomen
	belly
腹部	abdomen
腹肌练习	jackknife sit-up

改判	change of decision
改善	improve
改正	correct
盖帽拦网	capped block
干扰	distract
	interfere
	interfering
赶上	overtake
钢丝	cable
杠铃	barbell
杠铃片	disk
杠铃重量	weight of the barbell
高点击球,高点扣球	high spike
高点平扣	high flat shot
高吊球	lob
	lobbing service
高度	height
高发球	sky serve
	ceiling service

高平传	high flat
高球	lob
高速度	fast
高抬腿伸展	high knees
高校比赛(大学)	college tournament
高压吊球	power dink
高一点	nice
高于球网上沿	above the top of net
隔幕接球	screen receive
个人发球掩护	individual screen
个人技术	individual skills
	individual tactics
	individual technique
个人进攻	individual offense
个人警告	personal warning
个人时间差进攻	one-man time difference attack
个人掩护	individual screen
个人战术	individual tactics
各种各样的	various
给	give
给出	hand out
给分	award

跟腱拉伸	achilles stretch
跟进	run in
	follow in
	trai
跟进队员	follower
	trailer
跟进防守	"man-up" defense
跟随	follow
更衣室	changing room
	dressing room
工作周期	cycle of work
公斤	kilogram
公正的比赛	fair play
弓箭步	forward lunge
攻防转换	transition
攻防转换模式	transition patterns
攻防转换训练	transition drills
攻击力	attack ability
攻击区域	attack block
攻击手	attacker
	attack man
	spiker

攻击线,进攻线	attack line(s)
攻击性发球	offensive service
攻击性击球	attack shot
攻击性拦网	offensive block
攻击训练	attack drill
攻球	attack
攻手	attacker
	attack man
	spiker
攻线脚断	attack-line foot-fault
共同练习	joint practice
供给	feed
勾飘	Japanese service
	hook float
勾手	hook
勾手大力发球	cannon-ball service
	windmill smash
勾手发球	hook serve
	hook service
	roundhouse serve
	windmill serve
勾手扣球	hook smash

	hook spike
	roundhouse spike
	windwill attack
够	reach
够不着	out of reach
够得着	within reach
股四头肌伸展	quadriceps stretch
骨干	backbone
骨骼	bone
	skeleton
故意拖延比赛	intentional delay of the game
挂网的网绳	cable
观察扣手	reading the spike
关闭	close up
	off
关键	cues
	key
关键时刻	a critical moment
关节	joint
官员	match official
	officials
贯穿节奏	pacing

冠军	champion
	first
冠军杯	champion cup
规定	prescriptions
规则	rule
规则实施	rules enforcement
规则委员会	rules of the game commission
轨迹	trajectory
诡计	trick
跪垫	kneeling dig
滚动	roll
滚动传球	rolling volley
滚动垫球	rolling dig
滚动救球	rolling retrieve
滚翻	roll
滚翻垫球	rolling dig
滚翻救球	rolling receive
滚网球	net ball
国际奥委会	International Olympic Committee
国际比赛	international competition
	international match
国际裁判	international referee

国际裁判委员会	International Referee's Commission (IRC)
国际裁判学习班	international referee courses
国际裁判员训练班	international referee courses
国际的	international
国际翻译协会	Federation Internationale des Traducteurs(FIT)
国际规则	international rules
国际规则委员会	Rules of The Game Commission (RGC)
	International Arbitrage Commission (IAC)
国际候补裁判	international referee candidate
国际教练委员会	international coaches' commission
	international coaches committee
国际教练学习班	international coaches' courses
国际教练员训练班	international coaches courses
国际联合会	international federation
国际排联	Federation Internationale Volleyball(FIVB)
国际排联控制委员会	control committee of FIVB
国际排联行政会	Board of Administration of FIVB

国际排球联合会	FIVB
国家奥委会	National Olympic Committee
国家队	national team
国家级裁判	national referee
国家联合会	national federation
国家男队	men's national team
国家女队	women's national team
国家青年队	junior national team
国家协会	national association
腘绳肌伸展	hamstring stretch
果断的移动	assertive movement
裹住球	wrap over the ball
过程	training process
过度紧张	overstrain
过度运动	excessive exercise
	over-exercising
过渡	transition
(起跳时)过渡到脚掌	rocket over onto the toes
过渡期,过渡区	transitional period
过头传球	overhead pass
过头传球站位	overhead pass position
过头发飘球	overhead float serve

过头救球	overhead dig
过网	over the net
过网犯规	foul over the net
	reaching beyond the net
	interference
过网区	passing space
	crossing space
过线	over the line
过中线	off-side
过中线犯规	court penetration

海马区	hippocampus
毫无威胁的进攻扣球,能够让防守一方组织防反	free ball
好	good
	well
好球	good
号码	number
	numbering
号码牌	numbered card
合成地板	synthetic floor
合成地面	synthetic surface
合法比赛间断	legal game interruption
合法的	legal
合法发球	good service
合法间断	legal interruption
合法替换	legal substitution
合法暂停	legal time out
合格的	eligible

合作	cooperate
和解	accommodation
核对位置	position checking
黑马	dark horse
横跨步跑	side steps running
横向水平运动	lateral movement
红牌	Red
	red card
后	back
后摆动作	swing to the rear
后场	backcourt
后场出界线	baseline
后场防守	backcourt defense
后场防守策略	backcourt defense strategies
后场防守技术	backcourt defense techniques
后场平行传球	backcourt set
后场区	back court
	back zone
后撤	withdraw
后撤步	drop step
后蹬	takeoff drive
后蹬跑	driving leg running

后滚	roll backward
后滚翻	back roll
(上衣)后号码	back number
后交叉进攻	rear switch attack
后排	back row
后排保护	back up
后排传球	back row set
后排打法	back line play
后排队员	backcourt player
	back line player(s)
	back row player
后排队员进攻	back line player attack
后排队员进攻性击球	back-row plyer's attack-hit
后排二传队员	backcourt setter
	back row setter
后排跟进	penetration
后排跟进保护	back up
后排攻	backcourt attack
	backcourt spike
	backline offense
后排进攻	back attack
	back row attack

后排进攻队员	back court spiker
后排进攻攻防转换	transitioning for back-row attack
后排平行传球	backcourt set
后排替补队员	back-row sub
后排位置	back court position
后排右(一号位)队员	back right
后排中(六号位)队员	back center
后排专门防守	back-row specialist
后排阻拦训练	back row drill
后区	back zone
后让	give
后卫队员设置	player back defined
后移	moving the backs
候补队员	substituter
候补国际裁判	international referee candidate
呼吸	breathing
呼吸调整法	breath control
弧线	curve
弧线助跑	curving approach
弧形高传球	loop pass
弧形高度	height of arch
壶铃	kettle-ball

互锁式握法	interlocking grip
护球	covering
护球区域	court area to cover
划臂拉伸	butterfly stretch
划臂练习	butterfly drill
滑	slippery
滑步	slide
滑铲攻击	slide attack
滑垒(棒球)	slide
滑轮	pulley
滑行拦网方法	go-slide blocking system
踝	malleolus
踝关节	ankle
	malleolus
还击	return
缓冲	give
缓冲动作	action of giving
	amortization
	giving action
换发球	change of service
	side-out
	side out

换人	substitute
	substitution
换人犯规	substitution foul
换人请求	substitution request
换人区	substitute's area
	substitution zone
换人暂停	time-out for substitution
换位	replace
	switch positions
	switching
黄牌	yellow card
晃传	feint set
晃拦网	confusing the block
晃跳	cover jump
	trick jump
挥臂	arm swing
	swing
挥臂速度	arm speed
挥动	wave
恢复	recovery
恢复期	cooling period
恢复时间	recovery time

hui

回	return
回传	return
回复时间	recovery time
回合	rally
混合技术	miscellaneous techniques
混合跳发球	hybrid jump serve
混凝土地板	concrete floor
活动性游戏	gamelike exercise
获胜场次	game won

IR 制服　　　　IR uniform

J

J 型传球	J stroke
	scoop
击,击中,命中	hit
击球	hit
	hit the ball
击球出界	shoot out the ball
击球的异侧手臂	non-hitting arm
击球点	hitting point
击球区	hitting zone
击球入网	hit the ball in the net
击球者	hitter
击入空当得分	score a placement
机动的	maneuverable
机构	body
机会	chance
机会球(对方处理球)	chance ball
	easy ball
	free ball
机智	wit

肌肉	muscle
肌肉爆发力	muscle power
肌肉紧张	tense
肌肉力量	muscular strength
肌肉耐力	muscular endurance
肌肉强度	muscular strength
积分板	score a placement
积极主动的队员	active player
积累分数	running score
基本词汇	fundamental terminology
基本的	basic
基本防守站位	basic defensive position
基本功	basic fundamentals
	basic skills
基本攻击	basic attack
基本技能	basic skills
基本技术	fundamentals
基本位置	basic position
基本形式	basic form
基本训练	basic training
	fundamental training
基本原则	fundamentals

基本站位	basic position
基本阵形	basic formation
基本阵型	basic formation
基本姿势	basic form
基础的	basic
基础技术训练	basic skill training
基础进攻	basic attack
基础训练	fundamental training
激动	emotionality
及格赛	qualification match
极限	limit
急起	rocket start
急速	flick
急速发力动作	flick
急停	quick stop
疾跑	dash
集体防守	team defense
集体进攻	combination attack
	team offense
集体精神	team spirit
集体拦网	collective block
	combination block

	group block
	multiple blocks
集体配合	team work
	team up
集体配合打法	team play
集体行动	team action
集体掩护	collective screen
集体意识	group consciousness
集体战术	group tactics
	team tactics
集训制度	squad system
集中	concentration
集中点	convergence
集中战术	hut
集中注意力	focus attention
挤	hustling
计分	score
计分员	scorer
计划	program
计时	timing
计时比赛	timed games
计数	count

记分	point
记分板	score board
记分表	match sheet
	score sheet
记分方法	scoring system
记分员	scorer
	score keeper
记录	score
记录表	score sheet
记录台	scorer's table
记录员	scorer
记住	keep in mind
纪律	discipline
纪念章	badge
技能	ability
	skills
技能水平	ability level
技术、技巧	technique
	skills
	technical skills
技术成分	technical elements
技术串联	combination of techniques

技术错误	technical error
	technical mistake
技术的	technical
技术犯规	technical foul
技术水平	ability level
	technical level
技术统计	stroke analysis
技术委员会	technical commission
技术训练	technical training
技术要素	technical element(s)
技术员	technician
技术暂停	technical time-out
季节	season
季中回顾	midseason review
加入	enter
	join
加速	accelerate
	speed up
加速度	acceleration
加速力量	accelerating force
加速跑	accelerative running
	pick-ups running

加油,快!	come on!
夹臂	arm lock
夹塞	wedge-in attack
	in-side tandem
	squeeze attack
夹塞进攻	wedge-in attack
甲级	first class
	first division
假	fake
	feint
假布局	feint cover formation
假插上	feign move forward
	feint penetration of the setter
假传球	pass feint
假动作	deception
	feint
假交叉	fake cross
假交叉进攻	feint switch attack
假进攻	feint attack
假扣球	fake spike
	feint spike
假拦网	trick stop

尖子队员	top player
坚持	adherence
坚持下去	hold on
	play away stick to
	plug away
间断	interruption
间断的连续	sequence of interruption
间歇训练	intermittent training
	interval training
肩	shoulder
肩部伸展	shoulder stretch
肩绕环	shoulder roll
捡球员	ball-picker(s)
	ball retrievers
	retriever(s)
检测(鉴定)证书	control certificate
检查	check up
	test
检查表	check list
检查场地器材	check site equipment
	check playing court and facilities
健康水平	fitness levels

健康预期	fitness expectations
健身跑	jog
渐进放松法	progressive relaxation
渐进式阻力训练	progressive resistance
鉴定	judgment
箭步抓	split snatch
将球来回击打	volley
将球置于中心	centering the ball
讲习班	clinic
降低重心	keep low
交叉	across
	cross
	cross step
交叉比赛制	cross match system
交叉步	crossover step
交叉步跑	cross steps running
交叉步助跑	cross-over step approach
交叉进攻	cross attack
	fake cross
交叉拦网	crosscourt blocking
交叉拦网及防守线	blocking crosscourt and digging line

交叉配合	scissors movement
交叉赛	cross match
交叉训练	cross-training
交叉移动	crisscross
	scissors movement
交出	hand out
交换	change
交换场地	change of courts
交换场区	change of courts
交换发球权	change of service
	side-out
	side out
交换位置	change of position
	interchange of position
交替	alternating
角度	angle
角落	corner
角球	corners court
角运动	angular motion
绞车	winch
矫枉过正	beyond the limit of correction
	over-correction

jiao

脚,脚步	foot
脚步犯规	foot foul
脚的位置	feet position
脚法	foot work
脚跟触地	heel strike
脚跟到脚掌过渡	heel-toe contact
	rock over onto the toes
脚掌	ball of foot
	toe-ball
脚趾	toe
较轻排球	lighter-weight volleyball
教导	didactic
教法步骤	teaching progression
教练	trainer
教练法	coaching method
教练兼队员	player coach
教练委员会	coaches committee
教练员	coach
教练组	coaching team
教训	didactic
教育	education
接触	touch

接触球	contacts ball
接触球的位置	point of contact
接对方扣球	attack receive
接发球	receiving
	reception of service
	serve receive
	serve reception
接发球队	receiving team
接发球队员	receiving player
	serve receiving player
接发球失误	reception error
接发球体系	serve reception system
接发球替换	switching in receive
接发球一方	receiving side
接发球阵式	receiving pattern
接发球阵型	receiving formation
	serve reception formation
	serve-receive formation
接发球组合	serve-receive formation
接近	approach
接扣球	attack receive
	spike receive

接扣球练习	knock receive
	spike receive drills
接扣球阵型	attack reception formation
接球	receive
	receiving
接球方	receive side
接球失误	receive miss
接球直接过网	overpass
接受与承诺疗法	Acceptance and Therapy (ACT)
接受者	receiver
接应	support
接应二传	auxiliary setter
	co-setter
接应位置	support position
接应者	assist
节点分布	point distribution
节目	program
节奏	rhythm
	tempo
节奏和站位	tempos and locations
结果	result
结束	completion

截击	cut
	intercept
	volley
竭尽全力的	all-out
解除	release
解释	explanation
界内	ball in
	in
	inside
	inside the court
界内球	ball in
	ball "in"
	ball inside the court
	good
界外	ball out
	out
	out of bounds
	outside
界外球	ball "out"
	ball out
界线	boundary
	boundary lines

借助击球	assisted contact
	assisted hit
锦标	champion
锦标赛	championship
进场	march in
进场的队员	player that leaves
进攻	attack
	offence
	offense
进攻保护系统	attack coverage system
进攻成功	attack successful
进攻成功率	attack percentage
进攻次数	attack times
进攻打法	offense play
进攻得分	attack to score
进攻的	offensive
进攻的保护	attack coverage
进攻点	attack point
	point of attack
进攻队员	offensive player
进攻计划	game plans
进攻角度	attack angle

	cross-court
进攻力	attack ability
进攻路线	attack approach
进攻路线改变的地点	break point
进攻路线突然改变	break
进攻配合	attack combination
	offensive combination
进攻球员	hitter
进攻区	attack area
	attack zone
进攻失误	attack error
进攻受限方法	limited offense systems
进攻体系	attack system
	offensive system
进攻位置	offensive position
进攻系统	offensive system
	attack system
进攻线	attack line
进攻线前进攻	attack over the line
进攻行动	offensive action
进攻性击球	attack-hit
进攻性击球的完成	complete attack hit

jin

进攻性击球犯规	attack-hit foul
	attack hit foul
进攻训练	offensive drills
进攻意识	offensive minded
进攻战略	offensive strategy
进攻战术	offensive play
	offensive tactics
进攻者	attacker
进攻阵势	attack formation
	attack pattern
	offensive alignment
	offensive formation
	offensive pattern
进攻阵型	attack pattern
进入	entry
进入对方空间	into the opponent's space
进入对方区域	penetration into the opponent court
近体快球	one-set
	quick/A
	quick-A
	quick spike from close set

近网	close to the net
近网传球	close set
近网的	shallow
近网的传球	trap
近网二传球	close set
近网扣球	near-net-toss spike
禁止	forbid
精力	stamina
精确发球	precision serving
精神	spirit
精神不振	depression
精神紧张	mental strain
颈	neck
颈后负铃蹲跳	jumping on toes with bar on neck
颈后推	clean and press behind neck
警告	warning
径向偏差	radial deviation
净尺寸,使用面积	net size
净胜分	net points
胫骨前后轴	anteroposterior axis
竞技体育	competitive sport
竞技状态	competitive readiness

竞技状态良好	be in (good) form
竞技状态失常	out of form
竞赛	compete
	match
	tournament
竞赛地点	competition site
竞赛日程	competition schedule
竞赛与规则	competition and rule
竞赛制式	competition system
竞争	compete
静力半蹲	stationary squat
静力蹲	stationary squat
静力练习	static exercise
静力伸展活动	static stretching
静态平衡能力	static balance
纠正	correct
纠正错误	correction of error
酒精检验,酒精检查	alcoholic test
救得好	well saved
救起入网球	recovery from net
救球	dig
	get one's service in save

	recover
	recovery
	retrieve
救球补偿	dig to counteract
救入网球	net recovery
救网	net save
局	set
局点	game point
局间	interval
局间休息	interval between sets
沮丧	depression
举	raise
	lift
举臂	arm lift
	arm lifting
	arm raising
举起	lift
	raise
举球	lift
举球（违规的）	lifts illegal
拒绝	refuse
拒绝比赛	refuse to play

俱乐部冠军杯	club champion cup
距离	distance
决定	deciding
	final
决定胜负的进攻	winning attack
决赛	final
	final game
	final match
决赛名次	final standing
决胜	tie breake
决胜局	deciding set
	final set
	tie breaker
决心	determination
	fortitude
决战	showdown
角色	role

开	open
开放性练习	opening practice
开幕式	opening ceremony
开幕式上的比赛	opening game
开始	start
开始比赛	play ball
开始的位置	starting position
开始的阵型	starting formation
开始上场的队员	starting players
开始上场队员的号码	starting number
开始上场阵容	initial formation
开始阵容	starting line up
开始阵型	starting formation
开腿开立	astride straddle-stand
看	watch
看拦网	seeing the block
看着扣手	eyes on the spiker
扛杠举踵	toe raises
抗压强度	compressive strength

抗议	protest
靠边线的扣手	wing smasher
靠边线的拦网	wing block
靠近	close up
靠墙直立伸展	wall lean
靠头伸展	head lean
客队	visiting team
课程	course
课堂讲授	office coaching
空当	free space
	open area
	opening
	uncovered territory
	unprotected area
空间	space
空间差进攻	spike after flight forward
	space-shift attack
空位	seam
空中轻推	overhead dig
控制	control
	keep
控制发球	service control

控制方向	directional control
控制局面取得优势	dominate
控制拦网方法	control blocking systems
控制落点	placement
控制能力	control ability
控制球	ball handling
	control the ball
控制球!	control the ball!
控制区域	target area
	control area
扣	shoot
扣背快球	quick spike from backward set
扣背溜	quick spike from backward short
扣长线(底线)	deep shot
	long shot
扣集中球	close spike
	short set spike
扣近快	quick spike from close set
扣近网球	near-net-toss spike
扣空网球	open
	open spike
扣快球	quick spike

扣拉开球	open spike
	wide set spike
扣平拉开球	quick spike from flat wide set
扣球	attack
	hit
	kill
	slam
	smash
	spike
扣球保护	backing up the spiker
	covering the smash
	spike coverage
扣球变化	spiking variations
扣球成功	kill
扣球成功率	kill efficiency
扣球出界	spike out
扣球次数	attacking attempts
扣球的助跑	glide
扣球队员	attackers
	hitters
	spikers
扣球队员保护	spiker coverage

扣球后的自我保护	spike coverage
扣球后随球过网	reach over the net after the spike
扣球角度	hitting angles
扣球练习	knock
	spike drills
扣球路线	spike course
扣球区域	hitting zones
扣球失误	junk
	spike miss
扣球式发球	smash service
扣球手扣球前移动的扣球线路	slide
扣球手跑动后在离二传手一个身位处扣球	step-out
扣球手在二传手前一个身位扣球	step-in
扣球手在二传手周围一个身位扣球	step-around
扣球掩护	spike fake
扣入拦网手	spike in the block
扣杀	kill
扣手	attacker

	attack man
	hitter
	killer
	spiker
扣探头球	direct attack
	first time attack
	first hit to attack
扣调整球	spike with adjusting
扣"卧果"球	spick in the block
扣斜线球	crosscourt spike
	crosscourt attacks
	diagonal spike
扣远网球	far-net-toss spike
扣直线球	line spike
	line shots
	straight ball
跨步	stride
跨步式	lunge stretch
跨步下蹲	lunges
跨步助跑	step approach
跨步姿势	stride position
快	quick

	fast
快的	fast
快点	be quick
快攻	fast attack
	fast offense
	quick attack
	quick break
	quick offense
快节奏,快频率	fast tempo
快球	quick
	quick ball
	quick spike
	quick kill
快球扣杀	quick kill
快球训练	speed ball drills
快速传球	quick
快速反击	quick counter attack
快速进攻	high-speed attack
	quick attack
快速扣球	quick hit
快速起动	quick start
快一点	nice

kuan

宽度	width
髋	hip
髋屈肌伸展	hip flexor
困难(的)	difficult
扩散进攻	spread attack
扩音器	loudspeaker(s)

拉锯战	see-saw game
拉开传球	open toss
拉开扣球	open spike
拉力练习	lat pull downs
拉力器	lat machine
	Mini-Gyms
	weight pulley
拉开球进攻	open attack
拉三	widen 3
拉伸	cool down
拉四	widen 4
拉网选位	place the block
来回对打	rally
拦对方的扣球	block the spike
拦发球	service block
	block the service
拦回球	block rebounds
拦击	volley
拦截	intercept

lan

拦网	action of blocking
	block
	close up
	stop
拦网保护	block coverage
	stop cover
拦网步法	blocking footwork
拦网策略	blocking strategies
拦网成功	shut out
拦网得分	block point
拦网的保护	block coverage
	cover behind the block
拦网的空隙	gape in block
拦网的完成	completed block
拦网动作	action of blocking
拦网队员,拦网手	blocker
	stopper
拦网犯规	blocking foul or screening
	blocking foul
拦网封死的范围	block shadow
拦网覆盖的范围	shadow of the block
拦网换位	blocking shifts

· 126 ·

拦网技术	blocking techniques
拦网能手	blocking specialist
拦网区域	block area
拦网失误	block miss
拦网时触手出界	stop out
拦网时最有利的位置	zone block
拦网试图	block attempt
拦网手	blocker
拦网手的扣球	spike against the block
拦网未触球	block attempt
拦网位置	position of block
拦网线	blocking line
拦网选位	place the block
拦网战略	blocking strategy
拦网战术	blocking tactic
	blocking strategy
拦网遮蔽区域	block shadow
拦网遮盖区域	block shadow
拦网阵型	block formation
	blocking pattern
拦网直接得分	block point
拦网转移	blocking shifts

拦网准备击球姿势	exploding upward and pressing hands
拦网姿势	block form
拦住对方的进攻	spike off the block
捞	lift
	scoop
捞球	scooping
捞球动作	scooping
累积比分	running score
肋木	stall bars
冷静	sangfroid
冷静下来	cool down
冷却和拉伸活动	cool-down and activities
离开	off
离开场地	leave the court
离网	deep
离网传球	deep set
离网发球	serving from deep
力量	force
	strength
力量举	strength set
力量训练	strength training

	power training
	weight training
立体进攻	stereoscopic attack
立正	stand at attention
利用打拦网手反弹回来的打法	rebound play
连击	double
	double contact
	double hit
	dribbling
连击者	dribble
连续触及	consecutive contacts
连续触球	consecutive contacts
连续传球	consecutive passes
连续的	continuous
连续发球	continue to serve
连续犯规	consecutive fouls
连续接球	consecutive receive
连续扣球	consecutive spike
连续拦网	consecutive block
	consecutive blocking
连续请求	successive requests

lian

连续跳	running jump
连续训练	continued training
连续运动	constant movement
联合会	confederation
	federation
联赛	tournament
	tournament league system
联席会	general meeting
练习	drills
	exercise
	training
练习服	training suits
两臂间有空隙的双人拦网	split block
两步助跑	two-step approach
两次触球	double contact
两次球进攻	one-pass attack
	one-set spike
	one-two attack
	second hit attack
	second time attack
	two-attack

	two-step attack
两次球进攻的第一传	two-step toss
两次球扣球	two-count spike
两个队员的中间空档	seam
两名击球员防守轮转换位	two-hitter offensive rotations
两人打防	pepper drill with partners
两人一组练习	work in pairs
两人做熟悉球性联系	ball handling drills in pairs
两手都能扣球的队员	double attacker
两头翘	jackknife sit-up
两腿开立	astride
	striddle-stand
量尺	measuring rod
临场教练,临场教练员	bench coach
临场指挥	bench work
灵活的	maneuverable
灵活调整	acute adjustments
灵活性	agility
	flexibility
灵活战术打法	variation play
灵活战术的打法	variation of play

灵敏性	actuation ability
领队	manager
领先两分	a two point lead
	two point advantage
另外的	extra
六比二对抗组合	6 – 2 offensive
六比六对抗体系	6 – 6 offensive
"六二"进攻体系	6 – 2 offensive system
六二配备	6 – 2 system
六号位	center back
六号位队员	middle back player
六号位跟进队员	center up player
六号位压底队员	center back player
六人接发球阵型	six-man serve reception
录像	take video tape
录像带	video tapes
录像机	video recorder
路线	course
路线改变的地点	break point
路线扣球	line spike
挛缩	contractions
抡臂扣球	roundhouse spike

轮次转换	rotate
	rotation
轮次转换规则	rotation rule
轮换	alternation
轮换重叠	rotation overlap
轮换防守	rotation defense
轮换转换	rotational transition
轮流	alternating
轮转	rotation
轮转次序	rotational order
	serving order
轮转错误	error in the rotation order
	positional or rotational fault
轮转犯规,轮转次序错误	error in the rotation order
	rotational foul
轮转防守	rotation defense
轮转换位	rotation
轮转顺序	rotation order
轮转位置	rotational position
落地	landing
落点	landing point
落网球对落网球	down ball versus down ball

"M"阵型	M formation
马蹄形防守	two-four cover system
	half-moon defense
	hoof-shaped defense
马蹄形防守战术	perimeter
慢	slow
慢节奏	slow tempo
慢跑	jog
	jogging
慢速测试	moves off-speed test
慢速进攻	slow-speed attack
冒犯行为	offensive conduct
没有头脑	no-head
每球得分制	rally point
	rally point scoring
美国奥委会	United States Olympic Committee (USOC)
美国排球教练员协会	American Volleyball Coaches Association (AVCA)

美国排球联盟	USA Volleyball
美国排球协会	United States Volleyball Association (USVBA)
门诊所	clinic
猛冲,猛攻	rush
猛烈地	hard
猛推	thrust
迷	fan
"米卡萨"杯	Mikasa cup
密度	density
面	surface
面对	facing
面对球	facing the ball
面积	area
面斜打直	face crosscourt spike line
面直打斜	face line spike crosscourt
秒	second
秒表	stopwatch
	watch
敏度	acute
敏捷度系数	quickness factor
敏捷性	agility

名册	roll
名次	classification
	standing
	team standing
命中	hit
命中率	accuracy
抹	wipe off
抹拦网手	brush-off block
	wipe-off shot
抹球	wipe-off
抹球技术	wipe-off technique
木板场	wood court
木质地板	wooden floor
木质地面	wooden surface
目标	end
	mark
	target
目标发球	target serve
	target serving
目标区域	target area
目测范围	facing range
目的	object
目光接触球	eye contact ball

拿	take
耐久力	endurance
	staying power
耐力	endurance
	stamina
	staying power
耐力练习	endurance exercise
耐力训练	endurance training
难分难解	tie break
脑震荡	concussion
内撤保护	draw-in defense
	off-blocker defense
内收(作用)	adduction
内旋动作	medial rotation
能力	ability
能力测试	ability test
能力倾向	aptitude
能力倾向测试	aptitude test
能量维生素	energy vitamins

neng

能手	specialist
	technician
年龄	age
年龄组	age group
尿	urine
尿液分析	urine analysis
努力	effort

排	row
排球	volleyball
排球运动员	volleyballer
	volleyball player
排球阵营	volleyball camps
牌子	card
盘腿拉伸	pretzel stretch
判定	decision
判断	judge
	judgment
	judging
判罚	penalty
	penalization
	sanction
判罚出场	expulsion
判罚的等级	sanction scale
判罚的升级	the gradual application of sanctions
判罚等级	scale of sanction
判罚区域	penalty area

判给	award
判后回放	judgment call
旁线展示	sideline show
抛	throw
抛起	throw-up
	throw up
	toss up
抛球	toss
	toss the ball
"抛球"	throwing
抛硬币	toss a coin
跑	run
跑的练习	dash
	pace walk
跑动传球	setting on the run
	running set
跑动发球	running service
跑动防守	moving defense
跑动进攻	moving attack
跑动路线	runner's path
配备	matchups
配备站位进攻	in-system offense

配合	combination
	cooperate
	team up
配合打法	playing combination
配合进攻	combination attack
配合扣球	combi-spike
配合拦网	combination block
捧	lift
	scoop
碰	touch
碰到自由球	facing free balls
碰块	touch the block
批准	authorized
劈	cut
劈拦网手扣球	split the block
皮革	leather
疲劳	fatigue
	tired
	tiredness
骗局	trick
飘	float
飘动	float

	floating
飘动效果	floating effect
飘球	float
	floater
	slider
漂亮的垫球	nice set up
频率	tempo
平板拉伸	plank stretch
平传	parallel set
	parallel toss
	shoot set
平分,平局	tie
平衡点	balance point
平衡中心	center of balance
平弧度球	parallel set
	flat set
平静	calm
平拉开	shoot
	quick spike from flat wide set
	spike with wide low set
	parallel-long-toss quick ball
	four-set

平拉开传球	flat set
平拉开扣球	parallel-long-toss quick spike
平拉开球	shoot set
平手	tie
平行的	parallel
平移	type motion
评估	evaluation
评价	evaluation
屏障	screen
瓶塞	stopper
扑	rush-up

启动速度	starting speed
起动	start
起动速度	starting speed
起跳	take off
	take off drive
起跳的后蹬	take off drive
起跳点	take off point
起跳方法	method of take off
起跳脚	drive leg
气压	air pressure
	pressure
气压表	pressure gauge
气压计	air pressure gauge
弃权	default
弃权队	team in default
器材	equipment
	facilities
千克	kilogram
签字	sign

前臂	forearm
前臂传球	forearm pass
前臂垫球	forearm dig
前部,前面	front
前场垫球队员	front court diggers
前场区	front zone
前冲飘球	flat float
	flat-float service
前冲跳	forward flight
前传	front set
前传球	forward volley
前方二传	front set
前飞	forward flight
前滚	front roll
	roll forward
前交叉	right cross
	front switch attack
前交叉进攻	front switch kattac
前脚	advancing foot
前脚掌	ball of foot
	toe-ball

前进,前移	advance
前快	front slide
前快或背快传球	one-set
前排	front-row
前排队员	front line player
	front-line player
	front row player
前排队员进攻性击球	front-row player's attack-hit
前排进攻	front-row attack
前排平行传球	frontcourt setter
前排替补队员	front-row sub
前排位置	front row
前排线(即三米线)	10-foot line
前排右(二号位)队员	forward right
前排中(三号位)队员	center forward
	forward center
前排左(四号位)队员	forward left
前扑	sprawl
前区	attack area
	front zone
前外设置	front outside
前移动	forward movement

前鱼跃	forward dive
强度分级	gradation in
强队	strong team
强攻	force attack
	power attack
	shot
强力	force
强轮对强轮	diamond cut diamond
强势一方击球手	strong-side hitter
强制换人,强制替换	compulsory substitution
墙	wall
抢攻打法	aggressive play
抢攻打法阶段	stages of aggressive play
抢救	retrieve
抢救险球	ball retrieve
悄悄移动	creep
窍门	cues
	trick
切	cut
侵犯	invasion
侵犯行为	aggression
	aggression conduct

侵入防区	court penetration
青少年	youngster
青少年排球运动	youth volleyball
轻拨球	soft shot
轻拨球区域	tip zone
轻打	slow spike
轻吊	dink
	drop shot
轻扣	dink spike
	drop spike
	half speed hit
	off speed spike
	slow smash
	slow spike
	soft smash
	soft spike
	tip
	tipping
轻扣球	playing the tipper
轻扣球防守	defend off-speed
轻排球运动员	balloon volleyball
轻柔地	soft

轻视	underestimate
轻微不良行为的警告	misconduct warning
轻易打败	ease out
清楚	clear
清网	net clearing
清晰	clear
情绪	emotionality
请求	request
请求换人	request substitution
请求暂停	request time-out
	time out request
求战欲望	desire
球	ball
球霸	ball hog
球被触及	ball touched
球被拦后的反弹角度	rebound angle
球场	court
球从网下通过	ball crossing the lower space
球的触及	ball contact
球的飞行	flight of the ball
球的控制	ball control
	control of bal

球的气压	pressure of the ball
球的位置	position of the ball
球的旋转	rotation of the ball
	spin of the ball
球的运行轨迹	trajectory of the ball
球的重量	weight of the ball
球的周长	ball circumference
球兜	ball bag
球队	team
球队席人员	bench personnel
球落地前的预判移动	precontact position
球入网	in the net
	net in
球速	ball velocity
球太低,因而不能扣	too low to spike
球探报告	scouting reports
球通过球网时的犯规、球触及场外物体的犯规等	ball touched an outside object, or foot foul by any player during service
球网	net
球网尺寸	size of net
球网垂直面	vertical plane of net

球网垂直平面	vertical plane of the net
球网的底绳	cable of the net
球网的界外部分	outside part of the net
球网附近的球	ball at the net
球网附近队员	player at the net
球网钢丝绳	net cable
球网高度	height of net
球网滑轮	net pulley
球网检查	net inspections
球网界外部分	outside part or the net
球网上沿	top of the net
球网上缘	top of the net
	upper edge of the net
球网柱拉链	cable supporting the post
球网柱子	post
球衣	jerseys
球员得分记录表	box scores
球员对齐组合	player up formation
球员未对齐错误	player out alignment fault
球员站位	player position
球运行的轨迹	trajectory
区	zones

区域	area(s)
	zone
区域防守	field defense
区域拦网	zone block
驱逐出场	expulsion
驱逐某队员	expel a player
屈	bend(flex)
屈臂	arm bent
	bend arm
屈臂扣球	bent-arm spike
屈曲	flexion
屈身	bend
屈体前伸测试	sit-and-reach test
屈膝	bend the knee
	bending of knee
	knee bend
屈肘	elbow bend
躯干	torso
曲臂	bend arm
曲线	curve
曲线运动	curvilinear motion
取得控制权	getting in position

取位	get into the position
取消	cancel
	declare of
取消比赛资格	disqualification
取消资格	disqualification
	disqualify
	expulsion
权力	right(s)
全场防守	field defense
全队配合默契	team work
全国大学生体育协会	National Collegiate Athletic Association (NCAA)
全国少女和妇女体育运动协会	National Association for Girls and Women in Sport (NAGWS)
全力地	all-out
全面的,全能的	overall
全面身体训练	overall conditioning
全民运动	nationalism movement
全明星的	all-star
全能运动员	universal player
全身协调动作	total body action

拳	box
拳击球	punching ball
缺点	weakness
缺氧代谢	anaerobic metabolism
确认	confirm
群众比赛	mass tournament

RICE 法	RICE method
绕环	circumduction
绕肩伸展	shoulder roll
热身	warm-ups
热身场地	warm-up area
热身活动	warm up
热身及伸展运动	warm-up and activities
热增量	heat gain
人盯人拦网	man-to-man block
	man-to-man stop
人体防线	body line
人体运动学家	careers for body
任命名单	designation sheets
韧带	ligament
扔	throw
日本杯	Japan Cup
日本滚翻	Japanese roll
日本式发球	Japanese service
日程表	schedule

柔韧性	flexibility
柔软	soft
柔软的	flexibility
	flexible
	limber
柔软性	flexibility
入侵	invasion
入网球	ball in the net
	in-net ball
软障碍	soft block
弱	weak
弱点	weakness
	weak point
弱队	weak team
弱区	weak area
弱势传球者	weak passers
弱势一方的击球手	weakside hitter

赛点	match point
赛馆	hall
赛后	postmatch
赛后季节	post season
赛后评估	postgame evaluation
赛后谈话	postgame talk
赛季	season
赛间改变开场轮转换位	changing starting rotation between games
赛前	pregame
赛前的技、战术准备	technical-tactical preparation
赛前技术准备	technical preparation
赛前季节	pre-season
赛前介绍	pregame introductions
赛前身体训练	physical preparation
赛前事宜	pregame matters
赛前特别身体训练	special physical preparation
赛前团队会议	pregame team meeting
赛前训练	coaching before match

sai

赛前战术训练	tactical preparation
赛前准备	preparation of the match
三步进攻法	three-step attacking method
三步助跑	three-step approach
三差进攻战术	three-shifting tactic
三点进攻	three-hitter attack
三号位	center forward
三号位半高球的传球（在组织战术进攻时）	half lob of middle set chest-high ball of middle set
三号位半高球扣球	chest-high ball of middle spike half lob of middle spike
三号位单人拦快攻	one to one middle block
三号位副攻手扣半高球而二号位接应二传手掩护扣快球	the third position deputy attacker deducts the half-high ball and the second position picks up the setter cover buckle fastball
三号位或三号位的拦网队员	middle
三号位快球掩护拉开到二号位	No.3 fastball cover to open to No.2

三局两胜	best of three sets
三米线	attack line
	3-meter line
三名击球员防守轮转换位	three-hitter defensive rotations
三球制	three ball system
三人集体拦网	triple-block
三人接打球阵形	three-man serve reception
三人接发球阵型	three-man serve reception
	receiving on three line-up
三人拦网	three-man block
	triple block
三人压后防守	three-man deep defense
三人纵深防守	three-man deep defense
三人组合	three-player formation
"三三"配备	three-attack service reception
	three setter system
	three-three system
三头肌伸展	triceps stretch
杀球	kills
沙滩排球	beach volleyball
沙滩排球运动	beach volleyball

上背伸展	upper back
上臂	upper arm
上步	step in
上场	go on
上场阵容	starting line-up
上前	front
上身	upper body
上身训练	upper boby training
上升球	rising ball
上手	overhand
	overhead
上手传球	overhand pass
	overhead pass
上手传球很到位	accurate with forearm pass
上手二传	overhand set
	overhead set
上手发飘球	overhand floater serve
	overhead floater serve
上手发球	overhand serve
	overhead serve
上手发旋转球	overhand topspin serve
	overhead topspin serve

上手方式	overhand style
	overhead style
上手接发球方式	overhand serve-receive style
	overhead serve-receive style
上手飘球	overhand float
	overhead float
上手一传	overhand pass
	overhead pass
上体	upper body
上斜线打直线	line spike using a crosscourt approach
上旋	topspin
	overspin
上旋发球	topspin serve
上旋发球双手打法	hand contact for topspin serves
上旋球	outdrop
	topspin
上衣	jersey
上肢	upper limb
上直线打斜球	crosscourt spike using a straight approach
稍息	stand easy

哨	whistle
蛇形编排	serpentine system
	serpentine compiling system
设备	equipment
	facilities
设立标准	trap set
设施	facilities
射	shoot
申诉	appeal
	judical review game calls
伸	reach
伸臂长	arm's reach
伸臂滚翻救球	extension roll
伸出,伸展	outstretched
伸过	reach over
伸过球网	reach beyond the net
	reach over the net
伸展过度	hyperextension
伸展手臂	arm stretch
伸展训练	stretch training
伸肘	extended elbow
身材	stature

身长	body length
身份	standing
身份卡	identity cards
	I.D card
身高	body height
	height
	stature
身体	body
身体动作	body action
身体锻炼	physical conditioning
身体负重练习	exercise with weights strapped to the body
身体缓冲	giving of body
身体假动作	body feint
身体接触	physical contact
	body contact
身体前倾	lean forward
身体素质	constitution fitness
身体素质训练	fitness training
	conditioning exercise
身体素质状态	fitness
身体向前弯曲	pike

身体训练	physical training
身体训练(素质)	body building
	conditioning
	conditioning exercise
身体训练手段(方法)	conditioner
身体重心	center of body weight
身体姿势	body position
深的	deep
深度知觉	depth perception
深蹲	deep crouch
	deep knee-bend
	full squat
深蹲提踵	leg press toe raise
深蹲走	duck walk
神经肌肉特异性训练	neuromuscular specificity training
神经紧张	jitters
	nervous
神经战	battle of nerves
声明	protest
声音	sound
绳索	cord
胜	win

胜场	match won
胜负局的比值	game count
胜过	outstrip
胜局	set won
胜利	victory
胜一场	to win a match
胜一分	win a point
胜一局	to win a set
胜一局的关键	set point
胜一球	to win a rally
失	lose
失败场次	game lost
失发球	miss the serve
失发球权	lose the serve
	loss of service
	side-out
失球	lost ball
	miss the ball
失误	commit a fault
	error
	fail
	mistake

失误率	percentage of error(s)
失一分	loss of a point
失一局	lose a set
施力	force application
湿	wet
十项全能得分	decathlon scoring
十字	cross
十字交叉投球训练	criss cross drill
时间	time
时间差	pump
	delayed spike
	spike after delayed take-off
	one-man jikansa attack
	time differential play
时间差扣球	delayed spike
时间管理	time management
时间拉得很长的比赛	marathon match
识别速度及广度	speed and span of recognition
实力推	military press
实心球	medicine ball
实心球托球	medicine ball toss
实战情况下的训练	game situation training

拾球人	ball-picker
使……领先	put ... in the lead
使球上旋	producing a topspin
使用兴奋剂	doping
始终的节奏	pace
士气	spirit
示分牌	scorecard
世界杯	World Cup
世界杯赛	World Championship
	World Cup Competition
世界大学生运动会	the World University Games
	Universiad
世界冠军	world champion
世界锦标赛	World Championship
世界青年锦标赛	Junior World Championship
试图	attempt
视觉调节	accommodation
视力	vision
视频回放	video review
视野	view
适宜的规则	eligible rule
适宜性	eligibility

适应	adaptation
适应能力,适应性	adaptability
适应体育	adapted physical
室内	indoor
室内场地	indoor court
室内讲授	office coaching
室外	outdoor
室外场地	outdoor court
收腹	abdomen in
	abdomen flat
手	hand
手臂	arm
手臂鞭打动作	arm beat action
手臂拉过胸部伸展	arm pulls chest stretch
手臂前伸	arm straight forward
手臂圈伸展	arm circles stretch
手臂锁定姿势	arms in locked-out position (blocking ready stance)
手臂姿势	arm position
手的位置	hand position
手的姿势	hand position
手感	sense of hand-touch

手势	hand signal(s)
	signal
手势暗号	finger code
手势 25 红牌	hand signal NO.25 with red card
手势 25 黄牌	hand signal NO.25 with yellow card
手套滑垒训练	glove slide exercise
手腕动作	wrist action
手型	hand form
手掌	palm
手掌击球	bat the ball with palm
手指	finger
手指暗号	finger code
手指肚	pad of finger
手指扭伤	sprained finger
首次击球	first hit
首发阵容	lineup
首先发球	first service
受伤	injury
受伤程序	injury procedure
受伤的队员	injured player
授奖台	podium

授奖仪式	award ceremony
输	lose
输的队伍可以选择场地	the loser has the right to choose ends
输掉的比赛	lost game
数数	count
数据	data
数据分析	data analysis
甩腕	snap of wrist
	wrist snap
甩腕击球	flick at the ball
双	double
双插上配备	six-two system
双方持球	simultaneously held ball
双方触网	double touch-net
双方犯规	double foul
双方连续轮换发球	alternation
双方同时击球	simultaneous hit by opponents
双杠推起	parallel bars dip
双滑	double slide
双脚起跳	takeoff from both feet
	two-footed take off

双快（扣球手为二号位队员）	fake cross
	double quick
双快—跑动进攻	double quick and running attack
双快—游动	double quick swing
双人	double
双人传球练习	pass in pairs
双人（热身时）对打的练习	partner work
双人拦网	double block
	double close-up
	two-man block
双人拦网的"马蹄"防守	two-0-four cover system
双人拦网下的跟进防守	two-one-three defense system
双人拦网之外的拦网手	off-blocker
双人练习	partner exercise
双手传球	two hands set
双手垫球	forearms pass
	two hands dig
双手分持红＋黄	Red＋Yellow separately
双手接发球	two hands serve reception
双手同时犯规	simultaneous foul
双手头顶传球	overhead pass

双手协调	bimanual coordination
双手用力传出不带旋转的,力量角度恰到好处的球	toss
双淘汰制	double elimination system
双腿离地	double-leg takeoff
双腿伸展运动	groin stretch
双循环制	double round-robin system
双羽状的,双羽肌	bipennate
双轴的	biaxial
顺时针	clock-wise
顺时针轮转,顺时针方向轮转	clockwise rotation
顺手(近二传的手)扣球	on-hand spike
	on hand spike
(球)顺网滚动	run along the net
顺序	order
瞬间判断	split-second decisions
司线员	linesman
死角	dead corner
死球	ball out of play
	dead ball

	out of play
四次击球	four contacts
	four-hit
	four hits
"四二"保攻阵型	four-two spike coverage
"四二"国际进攻体系	international 4-2 offensive system
"四二"进攻体系	4-2 offensive system
"四二"配备	"4-2" system
	two-four system
	two-setter system
四分之一决赛	quarter finals
四号位	left forward
四号位队员向三号位移动跟随对方插上的队员的拦网战术	right-stack
四号位队员有计划地向三号位移动以跟随插上的进攻手	left-stack

si

四号位高拉开的强攻,四号位队员向对方快球队员移动和三号位的队员组成双人拦网的拦网形式,二传移动的动作	release
四号位进攻	four
四击	four hits
四人接发球阵型	four-man serve reception receiving on four-line-up
四人特别身体训练	special physical preparation
四人组队员	four-player formation
松劲	coast coast loose sluggish
素质测验	fitness test
素质练习	conditional exercise
速度	pace speed velocity
速度降低	loss of speed

速度扣球训练	speed spike training
速度慢而带有旋转的扣球	off-speed shot
速度训练	pace work
	speed training
速率	velocity
随队医生	team doctor
随球过网	follow through crossing the net
随意的	free
损伤	injury
锁定目标	goals and setting
锁定手肘	elbows fully locked

踏	step
踏过	step over
踏过进攻线	step over the attack line
踏过线	step over the line
踏过中线	step over the center line
踏及	step on
踏及端线	touch the end line
踏及进攻	touch the attack line
踏进攻线	step on the attack line
踏线犯规	line foul
弹跳能力	jumping ability
弹跳训练	jump training
弹向	bounce (to)
弹性,弹力	elasticity
弹性垫子	cushion
弹震伸展	ballistic stretching
探头拦网	net block
躺	lie
淘汰	eliminate

	oust
淘汰赛	eliminatory match
淘汰制	elimination system
	knock-out system
特别裁判委员会	Special Refereeing Commission
特别裁判委员会会议	SRC meeting
特别裁制委员会	Special Officiating Commission (SOC)
特长	specialize
特定运动动作	exercise-specific actions
特殊规则	special rules
特殊拦网情况	special blocking situations
特殊替换	exceptional substitution
特殊训练	specificity of training
特邀裁判	invited referee
腾空	flight
腾空高度	height of arch
腾空阶段	flight phase
腾空接球	flying receive
腾起	lift
梯次	echelon
	tandem

梯次进攻	tandem attack
踢	kick
提高	improve
	raise
提铃至胸	clean the weight to the chest
	bring the barbell up to the chest
提升	elevation
提踵	heel raise
	lift the heels
	toe raise
体操	exercise
体后屈(展腹)	arch back
体力	body power
体能	fitness
体系	system
体线	body line
体育道德	sportsman-like
	sportsmanship
体育的	athletic
体育馆	gymnasium
体育协会	athletic association
体育运动	sport

体育运动管理人员	athletic administrator
体育运动俱乐部	athletic club
体育运动行为举止	sportsmanlike behaviour
体育运动组织委员会	sports organizing commission
体质	constitution
体重	body weight
体重指数	Body Mass Index (BMI)
替补	substitute
替补比赛	makeup match
替补队员	substitute player
	substituter
替补席	bench
	player's bench
	substitute's bench
替补运动员	substitutes
替换	substitute
替换队员	substitute player
替换区	replacement zone
"天鹅"练习(两头翘)	swan exercise
挑边	coin toss
	choice coin
	toss up

挑选	choice
挑选场地或球权	choice of court or service
条款	art.
	article
条例	protocol
条文	statute
调节幅度检查	push-up test
调整	adjustment
调整传球	adjusting set
	crosscourt set
	setting a deep pass
调整二传	adjusting set
跳	jump
跳背传	jump back set
跳触训练	jump and drill
跳传	jump pass
	jump set
跳传球	jump set
	jump pass
跳二传	jump set
跳发飘球	floater serve
跳发球	jump serve

跳起背传	jump back set
跳起传球	jump set
跳起大力发球	jumping power serve
跳起短传	short jump set
跳起二传	jump set
跳起发飘球	jump float
	jump floater serve
跳起发球	jump serve
跳起发上旋球	jump topspin serve
跳起发旋转球的方法	approach for jump spin serve
跳起攻击	jumping attack
跳起摸高	jump reach
跳起掩护	cover jump
跳上成躯体站立	jump stop
跳绳	rope jumping
跳跃	leap
跳跃训练	jump training
停止	stop
挺腹	belly arch
挺举	clean and jerk
通知	call (to)

同伴发球时站位轮次错误	overlap
同队队员	teammate
同队队员同时击球	simultaneous hit by two teammates
同排队员换位	lateral switch
同排换位	lateral switch
同时	simultaneous
同时触球,同时击球	simultaneous contacts
同向的	parallel
统计	statistics
统计分析	statistical analysis
头	head
头部转动伸展	head turn
头后臂屈伸	triceps extension
头上	over-head
头上传球	overhead pass
	overhead volley
头上二传	overhead set
投	shoot
投球上限	ceiling shots
投掷分析	throwing analysis
突破	penetration

突破拦网	pierce the block
突然动作	flick
突然袭击	surprise attack
团队导向目标	team-oriented goals
团队会议	team meetings
团队接力赛训练	team relay training
团队挑战训练	team challenge training
团结	unity
推	push
推动	shove
推动开展委员会	promotion commission
推攻	attack after free-ball ball reception
"推攻球"	free ball offense
推滑动作	shove-and-slide move
推起	pull-up
腿	leg
腿部爆发力	explosive leg strength
腿部运动	leg movement walking
腿的位置	leg position
腿后肌伸展	hamstring stretch
腿推器(综合练习器)	leg press

腿推提踵（举重）	leg press toe raise
退队	removal from team
退守	withdraw
退役队员	retired player
托起	toss up
托球	volley
拖把	mop
拖延	delay
脱轨攻击	derailing attacks
脱轨进攻	derailing attacks

"U"接发球阵型，"U"阵型　　U formation

W

"W"接发球阵型,W式进攻队形	W formation
"W"阵型	"W" pattern
	W formation
外侧拦网队员	outside blocker
外地比赛	out match
外观	surface
外界阻挡	outside blocker
外围传球	back outside pass
外线防守,周边防卫	perimeter defense
外形	form
外旋	outward rotation
外展(作用)	abduction
弯曲	bending
弯曲的	bent
弯屈	bend
完成	completion
完成某一项技术时身体的姿势	posture

完整动作	complete movement
玩	play
挽回	recover
晚跳	delayed take-off
腕	wrist
王牌	ace
网	net
网长	length of the net
网触队员	net driven into player
网带	horizontal band of the net
网的最上端	top of the net
网底绳	under rope
网高	height of the net
	net height
网钩	net hooks
网孔	mesh of the net
网宽	net width
网前队员	player at net
网前技术	play between the attack lines
网球式发球法	tennis-serve
网上得分	net points scored
网绳	cable

	rope
网绳脚轮	net winch
网下	under the net
网下穿越	penetration under the net
	space penetration
网下垂直平面	vertical plane under the net
网下空间	lower space
网眼	mesh
网柱	net poles
	net posts
	poles
	post
往下穿越	penetration under the net
微动关节	amphiarthroses
违反体育道德	unsportsmanlike
违规	violations
违规传球	irregular sets
违规的发球进攻	illegal attack serve
违规对准	illegal alignment
违规击打	illegal hit
违规替换	illegal substitution
违规运球	illegal dribble

违例	violations rule
伪装	fake
尾随	trai
委员会	commission
	committee
卫线	backline
为赢得比赛所需的优势分	advantage
未触手	no touch
未防范进攻	blind-side attack
未知错误	error in position
未知错误的处理	consequences of a positional fault
位置	position
位置表	line-up sheet
位置差进攻	spike after taking an extra step
	positional-shift attack
位置差扣球	alternate position spike
位置错误	error in position
	off-side
	out of position
	position foul
	wrong position

位置错误的处理	consequences of a positional foul
位置错误犯规	positional fault
位置交换	switch
位置移动	skip step
畏怯	timid
喂球	feed
温度	temperature
稳定性	stability
稳定状态	steady state
稳健准确	sureness
稳扎稳打	play safely
涡流区	vortex cavity
我的上手传球传得太高了	my forearm pass goes too high
我的下手发球对对方毫无威胁	my under-arm-serves are too easy for them to return
卧	lie
	lying down
卧推	bench press
	supine press
握踝滚翻	ankle roll
屋檐式拦网	roof

无发球权的一方	hand out
无法判断	judgment impossible
"无攻球"的防守	free ball defense
无配备站位进攻	out-of-system offense
无人防守的区域	unprotected
无人防守区域	unprotected area
无人拦网	open
无人拦网的攻手	loose man
	loose spiker
无人区	free space
无掩护进攻	open attack
无掩护扣球	open spike
无氧的	anaerobic
无氧适能	anaerobic fitness
无氧纤维	anaerobic fibers
无氧训练	anaerobic exercise
	anaerobic training
无氧阈值	anaerobic threshold
无氧运动	anaerobic activity
	anaerobic exercise
无氧运动爆发力	anaerobic power
无障碍空间	free space

无障碍区	free zone
无助跑扣球	standing attack
五一配备进攻体系	5-1 offensive system
五号位	left back
五局比赛	five-set games
五局三胜	best of five sets
五秒规则	five seconds rule
五球制	five ball system
五人接发球阵型	five-man serve reception
"五一"进攻体系	5-1 offensive system
"五一"配备	five-one system
	one centre
	one-setter system
物理疗法	physical therapy
物体	object

膝	knee
膝盖拉向胸部伸展	knee to stretch
系统	system
下沉	descend
下蹲	crouch
下蹲防守	crouch defense
下蹲式抓举	squat snatch
下蹲姿势	crouch position
下负重起踵练习	heel raise
下降	fall
下降期	falling episodes
下落	descend
	fall
下坡半蹲	half squats
下手	underhand
下手传球	underhand toss
	underhand volley
	underhand pass
下手垫球	underhand dig

下手发飘球	underhand floater serve
下手发球	underarm service
	underhand serve
下体	lower body
下旋	underspin
	backspin
下旋球	back spin
	underspin
下肢	legs
	lower body
下坠飘球	drop-float
	dropping float
夏威夷防守传球	Hawaii defend & set
先进的训练	advanced training
现代排球	modern volleyball
线	line
限制	limit
限制线	attack line
相邻块划分制	buddy system
相同轮换开场	starting in same rotation
向边线移动	outside
向后	backward

向后摆臂	backswing
向后传球	backward set
向后移动	backward movement
向拦网手扣球	smash on the block
向前	forward
向前传球	forward pass
向前动作	forward movement
向前伸直	extended straight forward
向前移动	forward movement
向上	upward
向上摆	upward
向上摆(臂)	upward swing
向网中间移动	inside
向下	downward
向下吊球	dropping to the floor
向下翻转练习	drop and drill
向心收缩	concentric contractions
向右看齐	right dress
	eyes right
向右转	right face
	right turn

xiang

向着对方半场的、斜线的穿越球	crosscourt
向左转	left turn
象征	emblem
削球	slice
小臂	forearm
小臂垫球	forearm dig
	bump
小边并列争球	small-sided scrimmages
小步跑	chopping of strides
小场地	small-size court
小场地练习	small-size game
小排球运动（四-四人）	Mini-volleyball
小旗	flag
小腿	shank
小腿屈伸	leg raises
小斜线进攻	sharp angled attack
小斜线扣球	sharp angled spike
	sharp angled attack
小心	take care
小型的并列争球	miniscrimmage
小运动量训练	light training

小运动量训练日	easy day
效果	effect
效力范围	effect scope
协调	coordination
	unison
协调合作很好的比赛	tight play
协调人	coordinator
协调性	coordination
协调员	coordinator
斜传球	cross pass
斜打	cuts
斜网传球	cross court pass
斜网助跑	diagonal approach
斜线	cross course
斜线垫球	digging crosscourt
斜线进攻	cross court attack
斜线扣球	cross court smash
	cross court spike
	cross smash
	cross spike
	diagonal spike
	oblique spike

斜线球	cross ball
	cross court
斜线助跑	diagonal approach
携带	carry
	carrying
鞋	shoes
心跟进	center up
	center follow-in
	center cover
	middle-in
心跟进防守	center cover defense
心跟进防守体系	center up defensive system
	No. 6 cover system
心理素质差	psychologically handicapped
心理训练	mental training
	psychological training
心理准备	psychological preparation
心情	mood
心身训练	psychosomatic training
心输出量	cardiac output
心脏复检	cardiac rehabilitation
心脏骤停	cardiac arrest

新手初学	beginner
信号	signal
兴奋	excite
兴奋剂鉴定	anti-doping control
	doping control
行动	action
	conduct
行为	conduct
行为犯规	conduct foul
行为准则	rules of conduct
性别检测	sex control test
性别检查	sex control
	sex test
性别鉴定	sex control
性别鉴定证明	sex control certificate
胸	chest
休息	rest
休息一会儿	have a rest
休息暂停	time-out
休整	cooling period
虚线	broken line
需氧代谢作用	aerobic metabolism

需氧的	aerobic
宣告比赛	call a play (to)
宣告犯规	call a foul (to)
旋转	spin
	turn
旋转球	spin
	curve
选拔	tryout
选拔赛	tryout
选拔赛时长	length of tryouts
选球权或场区	choice of service or court
选位	positioning
选择	choose
	selection
选择场地	choice of courts
选择发球权或场区	choice of serve or court
学习	learning
学习方法	learning method
血液兴奋剂	blood doping
循环	cycle
循环系统	circulatory system
循环(轮转)训练	circle drill

	circuit training
	cyclical training
循环制	round-robin system
循序渐进的训练	progressive training
训练	drills
	exercise
	practice
	train
	training
训练参数	training parameter
训练场地	training court
训练大纲	drill outline
	training program
训练的评估	training evaluation
训练法	training system
训练方法	training method
训练负荷	training load
训练计划	drill program
	training plan
训练进程	training process
训练进度	training schedule
训练课	training lesson

训练理论	theory of training
训练量	volume of training
训练模式	training pattern
训练期	training period
训练强度	intensity of training
训练设备	exercise equipment
训练员	trainer

压	press
压倒对方	overwhelm
压缩	compression
压线	on line
压线球	ball on line
哑铃	dumb bell
哑铃练习	dumb-bell exercise
亚排联	Asian Volleyball Confederation (AVC)
亚运会	Asian Games
亚洲式发球	Asian serve
亚洲运动联合会	Asian Games Federation (AGF)
延长比赛	push
延长空间	external space
延迟	tardiness
延期的比赛	postponed match
延伸	extension
延伸性	extensible
	extensibility

延误	delay
延误比赛	delay the game
延误警告	delay warning
延误判罚	delay penalty
严格训练	hard training
严密拦网	wall block
严重错误,严重犯规	major fault
颜色	color
掩盖,掩护	cloak
	screen
掩护进攻	wave attack
掩护扣球队员	feint spiker
掩护起跳	trick jump
掩护战术	feint tactics
验尿	urine analysis
佯攻	feint
	feint attack
	feint spike
	wave attack
佯攻队员	fake smasher
	feint spiker
仰卧起坐	abdominal curl

	abdominal raise
	sit-up
腰	waist
腰背部伸展	waist and back stretch
腰部	waist
腰部以上任何部位	any part of the body above and including the waist
腰腹部练习	belly button drills
邀请	invitation
邀请赛	invitation match
	invitational tournament
钥匙	key
业余	amateur
业余体育运动	amateur sport
一般犯规	minor foul
一般规律	common rule
一般进攻	general offense
一般身体训练	general fitness training
	general physical training
一般身体准备	general physical preparation
一般素质训练	general fitness training
一般性错误	general fault

一般运动	general motion
一步助跑	one-step approach
一步助跑起跳扣球	one-footed slide
一场比赛	match
一场比赛的决胜分数	match point
一场比赛结束	end of match
一场球	game
一传	first pass
一传不到位	poor first pass
一传到位	a good pass
一传队员	first passer
一传-二传-击球站位	pass-set-hit position
一传-二传-扣球	pass-set-hit
一传-二传-扣球站位	pass-set-hit position
一次扣球	direct smash
一次扣杀	direct spike
一次球进攻	direct attack
	first hit to attack
	first time attack
一次球扣杀	direct kill
一对一拦网	one-to-one block

一对一拦网战术(一名队员只负责拦对方一名队员)	stack-man
一对一训练	one-to-one drill
"一、二"报数	counting by two
"一、二、三"打法	set offense
一分领先	one point advantage
一个回合	rally
一个球,一分球,从发球到成死球	rally
一个铤而走险的二传动作。在队员的双手一起在脸前时,双臂弯曲,在脸前,前臂的后部接触球	reverse bump
一攻	first round attack
	serve receive attack
	serve-receive attack
一攻成功,直接得分	first time attack point
一攻有效	first time attack efficiency
一号位	right back

一号位队员	right back
一级联赛	division I
一局	a set
一局比赛结束	end of set
一局结束	set out
一局中决胜分数(局点)	game point
一球	rally
"一三二"接发球阵型	W and one service receive pattern
一英里步行测试	one-mile walk
医生	doctor
医务委员会	medical commission
仪式	ceremony
移动	move
	movement
	shift
移动防守	moving defense
移位	displacement
已出手的球	shot ball
已登记的队员	registered player
以智取胜	outthink
义务	duty
议定书(协议)	protocol

意识	consciousness
毅力	determination
	fortitude
因队员受伤的暂停	"injury" time out
因对方弃权而获胜	won by default
因弃权失败	loss by default
因球击网而网触队员	net driven into player
引体向上	chin-up
	pull-up
隐蔽	hid
英尺	foot
鹰眼挑战系统	challenge system
赢的队伍有发球权	the winner has the right to serve
影子射门训练	shadow shots training
应变能力	compliance
	coping ability
应变性	compliance
应对右侧进攻	facing right attack
应对中间进攻	facing middle attack
应对左侧进攻	facing left attack
应急技术	compliance

ying

硬	hard
硬场区	hard court
硬推	military press
	standing press
用更大力击球	hit it harder
用拳击球	fist ball
用手指吊球	soft spike with fingers
用掌击球	bat the ball
用左手的队员	left-hander
优点	advantage
优胜杯	winner's cup
优势	advantage
优秀队运动员	ace
优秀选手赛	masters tournament
优秀运动员	ranking player
游动防守	rotation defense
游动进攻	wave attack
游戏	game
	play
友好邀请赛	friendship invitational tournament
友谊赛	friendship match
有防守的区域	covered area

有快球和强攻的进攻	quick/shoot
有力的	powerful
有体育形象的	sportsmanlike
有体育作风的	sportsmanlike
有效	validity
有效的	effective
	valid
有效拦网	control block
	touch block
有效拦网后的地面防守	floor defense
有效杀球	kill efficiency
有效约束机制	active restraint
有氧代谢训练	aerobic training
有氧的	aerobic
有氧能力	aerobic capacity
有氧纤维	aerobic fibers
有氧训练	aerobic exercise
有氧运动	aerobic exercise
有氧运动耐力	aerobic endurance
有争议的球	disputed ball
右	right
右侧进攻	right side attcak

诱导练习,诱导训练	motivative training
鱼跃	dive
	fish dive
鱼跃救球	dive retrieve
	diving retrieve
	diving save
	recovery dive
娱乐排球	recreational volleyball
与网的距离	distance from the net
预备姿势,预备位置,准备站姿	ready position
预测	anticipate
	anticipation
预料	anticipation
预判	anticipate
	anticipation
预判对方的进攻战术,看对方二传的动作来判断球的走向和战术以组织拦网,后场六人防守	read
预判进攻	offense reading

预判拦网	block-read
预判拦网系统	block-read system
预赛	qualification round
预跳	jump in advance
预选赛	qualification tournament
原地扣球	standing attack
	standing spike
原地起跳	jump from standing position
	standing jump
原地起跳扣球	standing jump attack
原理	fundamental
	theory of training
圆锥跳	cone jumping
远网扣球	distance attack
	far-net-toss spike
跃	leap
越过	over
	across
越过进攻线	cross the attack line
越过进攻线进攻	attack over the line
越过球网垂直面	cross the vertical plane
越过球网的球	ball over the net

	ball crossed the net
越过中线	cross the center line
允许	authorized
	permit
允许发球	authorisation to serve
允许更换	authorized change
允许换人	authorized substitution
运动的	athletic
运动的形式	sports form
运动范围	range of sports
运动负荷	exercise load
运动会	games
运动技能	motor skills
运动科学	exercise science
运动量	amount of exercise
	amount of work
	training load
运动能力	athletic ability
运动能力测试	athletic ability test
运动区	exercise area
运动衫	shirt
运动伤害防护员	athletic trainer

运动上衣	jersey
运动生物力学	biomechanics
运动学	kinematics
运动训练	sports training
运动医学	sports medicine
运动语言	language of sport
运动员精神	sportsman-like
运动员位置	player's position
运动员训练教育认可委员会	Commission on Accreditation of Athletic Training Education (CAATE)
运动员资格审查委员会	Legal and Player's Qualification Commission
运动站立姿势	athletic stance
运动状态	state of motion

再来!	again!
在二传手和三号位队员之间半高球扣球	half lob spike chest-high ball spike half high ball spike
在二、四号位的二传手	wing setter
在界内	within bounds
在球网上缘	on top of the net
在……内	in
在……之后面	behind
暂短休息	a momentary rest
暂停	time-out
造成对方失误	make the faults
责任	duty
增强式训练	plyometric training
展开	deployment
战斗	fight
战斗精神	fighting spirit
战略	strategy

战术	tactic(s)
战术变化	variation of tactics
战术打法	tactical play
战术的	tactical
战术动作	tactical movement
战术二传	tactical set
战术方案	tactical plan
	tactical scheme
战术计划	tactical plan
战术进攻,有掩护的进攻	tactical play
战术扣球	combi-spike
	tactical smash
战术配合	combined tactic
	tactical combination
战术球	tactical ball
战术训练	tactical training
战术意识	tactical awareness
	tactical cognition
	tactical consciousness
战术阵型	tactical formation
	tactical pattern
站	stand

zhan

站队	line up
站立	stand
站位	positioning
站位对站位防守	position-versus-position defense
站位靠后的接发球队员	deep receiver
张开手传球	open hand pass
张开手掌	open hand
章程	statute
掌根	heel of hand
掌控能力	control ability
掌握	control
掌握时机	timing control
丈量	measure
障碍	blocking
障碍训练	blocking drills
召唤	call (to)
照明	lighting
	lumination
遮挡	hid
折体	bend in
折体跳	jackknife jump
折线	broken line

侦察	scouting
侦察对方,侦察对队	scouting the opponent team
真实的	real
阵容	line up
阵容不完整的队	incomplete team
阵式,阵型	pattern
	form
	formation
阵型最旁边的运动员	wing
镇静	calm
争论,争执	dispute
争球	scrimmage
争先赛	sprint
整场比赛	full match
整理活动	cool down
	final exercise
	warm-down
整体排球(全队配合打法)	combi-volley
整体战术布置和计划	game plan
正常比赛间断	regular game interruption
正面传球	face pass

	forward set
	front set
正面上手发球	tennis serve
正面上手扣球	tennis smash
正面双手传球	forward forearm pass
正面迎球的接发球	open up reserve
正确	correct
	right
正式比赛	official match
	official competition
正式的	official
正式仪式	official ceremony
支持	support
支援/后援角色	support roles
支柱	brace
知情同意书	consent form
执委会	executive committee
直	straight
直臂	extended arm
	straight arm
直臂扣球	straight arm attack
	straight arm spike

直的	straight
直接的	direct
直接得分	terminal contacts
直接得分的发球	ace
直接得分扣球	ace spiker
直接扣球	direct spike
直接拦网得分的球	stuff block
直立的手臂环绕	standing arm encircled
直立下蹲	standing squats
直上托球	topping toss
直踢腿	straight leg
直线	straight
	straight course
直线传球	line set
直线垫球	line digger
直线扣球	line spike
	straight spike
直线扣杀	straight kill
	straight smash
直线扣线	straight smash
直线球	line shot
	straight ball

	straight course
直线运动	rectilinear motion
职业疗法	occupational therapy
职业体育运动	professional sport
指导	director
	instruction
指导机会	coaching opportunities
指示	instruction
制动	arrestment
	brake
	step
	stop
制服	uniform
秩序表	schedule
秩序册	game schedule
	program
掷	throw
掷币	toss up
中部防守队员	middle blockers
中部击打队员	middle hitters
中场击球	hits in the middle
中场扣球	spikes in the middle

中断	interruption
中国队发球,美国队准备接球	China serves, American gets read
中国式打法	Chinese style play
中间的	middle
中间队员	center player
中间击球手	middle hitter
中间拦网	center block
中间拦网队员	center blocker
	center block player
	middle blocker
中立场地	neutral court
中路	middle line
中枢性疲劳	central fatigue
中速进攻	medium-speed attack
中下部	lower part
中线	center line
	midline
中线穿透	enter line penetration
中心	center
中心线	center line
中央的	central

"中一二"进攻阵型	setter-in-FC formation star-like position offense
"中一二"阵型	setter-in-FC formation
	setter-in-FC formation star-like
终结	end
终止的比赛	broken plays
踵	heel
仲裁	jury
仲裁成员	members of jury
仲裁会议	jury meeting
仲裁委员会	jury committee
	arbitration committee
重点进攻区域	primary target area
重点拦网区域	overloading blocking zone
重扣	hard spike
重力	force of gravity
重量,重	weight
重心	balance point
	center of balance
	center of gravity
周边视觉	peripheral vision
周长	circumference

周期	cycle
周期训练	cyclical training
周训练计划	weekly training schedule
洲际联合会	Continental Confederation
轴	axis(Ax)
轴向力	axial force
肘	elbow
肘弯屈	bending at the elbowz
肘形弯管	elbow bend
主裁	director
主裁判	referee
主动	initiative
主动攻击模式	aggressive style
主动肌	agonist
主动脉	aorta
主动性伸展	active stretching
主队	home team
主二传	first setter
	main setter
	specialist setter
主攻队员	main attack player
主攻攻防转换步法	transition footwork for attackers

主攻手	ace spiker
	main-spiker
	power hitter
主攻手接触	spiker contact
主攻手进攻	spiker attack
主攻手拦网进攻	attack by a hitter block
主攻手自己托球并扣球	pass-and-hit control
主观性目标	subjective goals
主拦队员	block leader
	main blocker
主力、核心	backbone
	backbone core member
主任	director
主要二传手	special setter
助攻	assist
助拦队员	assistant blocker
助理	assistant
助理教练	assistant coach
助跑	approach
助跑发球	running serve
	running service
助跑方向	direction of approach

助跑起跳	running jump
助跑起跳扣球	running jump spike
助手	assistant
注意	pay attention to
	watch
注意!	watch!
注意力集中	focus attention
柱	pole
抓举	snatch
抓住	carrying
专家	specialist
专位防守	stationary defense
专项身体训练	special fitness training
	specil physical training
专项速度	specific speed
专心	concentration
专一	single
转动	rotation
转动臀部	hip turning
转队	transfer
转队证明	transfer certificate
转肩伸展	shoulder turn

转扣,吊扣	dink spike
转身	body turn
	turn
转体	body turn
	body twist
	turn
	turn the body
转体动作	body twist
转腕	turn the wrist
	wrist rotation
	wrist turn
转移	transition
装置	set
状态良好	in (good) form
状态失常	out of form
撞击	bump
撞球	miscue
追分(当比赛落后时)	chase points
追踪点,追踪分数	tracking points
准备	get ready
	preparation
准备动作	preparatory movement

准备会	preparatory meeting
	team meeting
准备活动	warming-up
	warm up
	limber-up
准备活动程序	warm-up routine
准备活动区	warm-up area
	warm-up zone
准备期	preparation period
准备位置	preparatory position
准备行为	preparatory activity
准备姿势	preparatory position
准确度	accuracy
捉肘	lift the elbow up
资格	qualification
资格赛	qualification match
资料	data
姿势	form
	position
	posture
自传并击球给队友	self-toss and hit to partner
自动弃权	voluntary default

自然运动	naturalism movement
自我分析	self-analysis
自我控制	self-control
自我认知	self-knowledge
自我掩护	self-feint
自我掩护战术	self-feint tactic
自由的	free
自由的判决风格	laissez-faire officiating
自由防守队员替换	replacement
自由球	free ball
自由球员	libero
自由区	free zone
自由人	libero
	the libero player
综合训练	combined training
综合战术	combined tactic
总管	manager
总教练	head coach
纵跳	vertical jump
纵跳摸高	jump and reach
	jump reach
走	walk

足	foot
足屈	plantar flexion
阻碍犯规	interference foul
阻力训练	resistance training
组	group
组成拦网	form the block
组次	sets
组合	combination
组合动作	joint motion
组委会	organizing committee
组织进攻	set up
	set up an offense
	set up on offense
组织进攻队员	game maker
	play organizer
组织者	organizer
最大负荷	maximal load
最大吸氧量	maximal oxygen
最大自由球	free-ball max
最后报名	final entry
最后判定	final decision
遵守	abide

左	left
左侧队员	left player
左路进攻	left side attack
左右晃动	move sideways
作用	effect
	role
作用力,外加力	applied force
坐	sit
坐式排球	sitting volleyball
做好准备	get ready
做几节操	do some exercises
做记录	keep record

附 录

附录1 生活用语

癌症是一种致命的疾病	cancer is a deadly disease
爱屋及乌	love me, love my dog
安静点	be quiet
吧台	counter
白酒	liqueur
白兰地	brandy
白兰地杯	brandy glass
白忙了	the answer is zero
白葡萄酒	white wine
百家得	bacardi
百事可乐	pepsi cola
百威啤酒	budweiser
帮帮我	give me a hand
棒极了	it's awesome

包你满意	your satisfaction is guaranteed
保持联络	keep in touch
保重	take care
贝克啤酒	beck's
被人批评真是痛苦	being criticized is awful
比利酒	bailey's
必须想个办法	something must be done about it
闭嘴	shut up
标记	logo
别吵了	stop making such a noise
别出差错	don't make any mistakes
别担心	don't worry
别放弃	don't give up
别紧张	take it easy
别客气	help yourself
别瞒着我事实真相	don't keep the truth from me
别谦虚了	don't be so modest
别让我失望	don't let me down
别上当	don't fall for it
别误会我	don't get me wrong
别这么孩子气	don't be so childish
别这么谦虚	don't be so modest

别指望我	don't count on me
冰勺	ice scoop
冰勺夹	ice tong
冰箱	refrigerator
波尔多红葡萄酒	claret
菠萝	pineapple
薄荷	mint
不必客气	don't mention it
不管怎样还是要谢谢你	thank you all the same
不合常理	it doesn't make sense
不会花很多时间	it won't take much time
不劳无获	no pain, no gain
不劳则无获	no pain, no gain
不是你的错	it's not your fault
不行	no way
不许动	don't move
不要急于下结论	don't jump to conclusion
不要惊慌失措	don't lose your head
不要碰运气	don't trust to chance
不要让机遇从我们身边溜走	don't let chances pass by
不要让我等得太久	don't keep me waiting long

不要为此灰心丧气	don't let this get you down
不要想当然	don't take it for granted
不要心存侥幸	don't take any chances
不要虚度光阴	don't dream away your time
不要在舞会上挥动手臂	don't swing the arms at ball
不要坐失良机	don't miss the boat
不要做无益的后悔	don't cry over spilt milk
不用麻烦了	don't bother
不用找了	keep the change
不足挂齿	it's nothing
餐前葡萄酒	appetizer
餐厅,餐馆	restaurant
草莓	strawberry
迟到总比不做好	better late than never
床单不能换	the sheet can't be changed
吹牛	talk big
春天是一个好季节	spring is a pretty season
错过的机会永不再来	a lost chance never returns
打不通电话	I couldn't get through
打印	print
代表我向你们全家问好	give my best to your family
但愿我能	I wish I could

但只有一点	but just one point
当然可以	certainly
当然了	of course
当然是	absolutely
当心	watch out
到目前为止还好	so far, so good
到时候见了	see you later
登记	check-in
等一等	hold on
等着瞧	just wait and see
电动搅拌机	electric blender
丁香	clove
订	order
订餐	ordering food
冬天是一个寒冷的季节	winter is a cold season
都是我的错	it's all my fault
都一样	it doesn't make any difference
杜松子酒	gin flzz
对不起	excuse me
对不起,我迟到了	I'm sorry I'm late
对此我非常抱歉(遗憾)	I am so sorry about this
对这件事我不觉得后悔	I felt no regret for it

多谢合作	thanks for your cooperation
发牢骚没什么用	it's no use complaining
发生了什么事	what happened
发生了一些事	something's come up
法国白兰地	cognac
凡事都有开端	everything has its beginning
房间钥匙	room key
放手	let go
非常感谢	thank you very much
	thanks a million
吠犬不咬人	a barking dog doesn't bite
风暴使树木深深扎根	storms make trees take deeper roots
伏特加	vodka
福士啤	foster's
该吃晚饭了	it's time for dinner
赶快	come on
感谢你的邀请	I appreciate your invitation
感谢你做的一切	thank you for everything
橄榄	olive
高脚杯	goblet
高粱酒	kaoliang spirit
高兴起来	cheer up

哥顿	gordon's
格兰菲迪	glenfiddich
隔墙有耳	the wall has ears
给你	here you are
给我打电话	give me a call
跟我来	follow me
柜台	counter
果汁榨汁机	juice extractor
过会儿再来找我	catch me later
过去的,就让它过去吧	let bygones be bygones
过去的痛苦即是快乐	pain past is pleasure
还不错	not bad
还没	not yet
好吧	all right
好吃的	tasty
好得难以置信	it's too good to be true
好久不见	it's been a long time no see
	long time no see
好主意	a good idea
很高兴能和你一起工作	so glad to work with you
很高兴认识你	it's nice meeting you
很高兴听你这样说	I'm very glad to hear that

很难说	it's hard to say
很受欢迎的菜	it's a most popular dish
红葡萄酒	red wine
湖	lake
护照	passport
滑冰很有趣	skating is interesting
皇冠	crown
黄瓜	cucumber
黄酒	rice wine
恢复播放	resume the play
徽记	logo
火车准时到达	the train arrived on time
几乎说不出话来	hardly speak
机不可失,时不再来	opportunity knocks but once
鸡尾酒	cocktai
记住它	remember it
加士伯啤酒	carlsbery
简洁是智慧的精华	brevity is the soul of wit
简直太棒了	just wonderful
健力士啤酒	guinness
捷足先登	first come, first served
解决	settle

今天是个好天	it's a fine day
今天天气很好	it's a nice day today
金酒	gin
金钱不是一切	money is not everything
金窝,银窝,不如自己的草窝	east, west, home is the best
紧紧跟随	follow closely
尽力而为	try my best
禁止在大街上吐痰	no spitting on the street
景色	scenery
酒吧	bar
酒吧男招待	barman
酒吧女招待	barmaid
酒吧椅	bar chair
酒壶	flagon
酒钻	corkscrew
就读给我听好了	just read it for me
就是这么回事	that's the way it is
就在附近	just around the corner
就这样	that's all
就这样吧	just let it be
桔子水	orangeade

桔子原汁	orange juice
距离	distance
绝对不可能的	absolutely impossible
绝对地	absolutely
绝对如此	absolutely
开瓶刀	bottle opener
看来这没问题	it seems all right
看情况	that depends
可得到的	available
可口可乐	coca cola
可能吧	probably
可以	that's OK
恐怕这事我干不了	I'm not sure I can do it
矿泉水	mineral water
来吧	come on
来得容易，去得快	easy come easy go
来这里	come here
郎姆酒	rum
量杯	measuring glass
量酒器	pouring measure
两个人都没说过话	neither of the men spoke
领房间钥匙	room key collection

令人难以置信、不可思议	it's incredible
马提尼红/干/白	martini rosso,dry,blanco
马提尼酒	martini
慢点	slow down
慢慢来	take your time
没关系	that's all right
没什么区别	that makes no difference
没时间了	time is running out
没问题	no problem
没有人知道	no one knows
美味的	tasty
密西西比(美国州名)	Mississippi
明天放假	tomorrow will be a holiday
莫依赖明天	tomorrow never comes
那可提醒我了	that reminds me
那可以理解	that makes sense
那么我只拿我所需要的东西	so I just take what I want
那没问题	that's not a problem
那事使我颇感惊讶	it rather surprised me
那是不对的	that's not true
那是毫无疑问的	there is no doubt about it

那是肯定的	that's for sure
那是值得的	that's worthwhile
那太好了	that's good
那太荒唐了	that's ridiculous
那听上去是个好主意	that sounds like a good idea
那样才像话	that's more like it
那样公平	that's fair
那谣言没有根据	the rumor had no basis
那与我无关	I have nothing to do with it
那再好不过了	that couldn't be better
耐心点儿	hold your horse
你拨错电话号码了	you've dialed the wrong number
你不跟我们说点什么吗	don't you speak something to us
你不可好高骛远	you mustn't aim too high
你的立场错了	your position is wrong
你的眼力不错	you've made a good choice
你的状况会好起来的	you will be better off
你得等一等看	you will have to wait and see
你该知足了	you can't complain
你干得很好	you did a good job
你会习惯的	you'll get used to it
你开玩笑吧	you are kidding

你可以指望我	you can count on me
你买得真便宜	you got a good deal
你没错,他也没错	neither you nor he is wrong
你们最好是让她一个人呆会儿	you'd better let her alone
你明白了	you've got it
你能得到你想要的	you can get what you want
你能做到	you can make it
你确定	are you sure
你说得有道理	you've got a point there
你说得挺有道理的	you've got a point there
你算说对了	you said it
你完全正确	you are quite right
你喜欢我就高兴	i'm glad you enjoyed it
你想得真周到	it's very thoughtful of you
你想要什么	what do you want
你想知道什么	what do you want to know
你需要的就是休息	what you need is just rest
你需要休假	you need a vacation
你也一样	the same to you
你应该好好利用这个机会	you should take advantage of it

你应该试一试	you should give it a try
你早就该睡觉了	it's time you went to bed
你真有心	you are so considerate
你知道这对我的工作是必要的	you know it's necessary for my work
你只是说说而已	you are just saying that
您先	after you
柠檬	lemon
柠檬水	lemonade
柠檬原汁	lemon juice
哦,你别拿我开玩笑了	oh, you are kidding me
啤酒	beer
啤酒杯	beer mug
平底无脚酒杯	tumbler
苹果酒	calvados
瓶	bottle
葡萄	grape
葡萄酒杯	wine glass
签名	signature
签字	sign
琴酒	gin
清真	Moslem

	Muslem
	Muslim
情况正在好转	things are getting better
请把菜单给我	please show me the menu
请便	be my guest
请别打扰我	please leave me alone
请别客气	please make yourself at home
请不要拘礼	make yourself at home
请不要责怪你自己	please don't blame yourself
请出示你的票	show your tickets, please
请多保重	take care
请告诉我一声	please let me know
请给我来这个	please give me this one
请接受点菜	please take my order
请接受我的道歉	please accept my apology
请进,别客气	come in and make yourself at home
请慢慢享用吧	enjoy your meal
请你原谅	I beg your pardon
请原谅我	forgive me
请自己用	help yourself, please
取	fetch
	go and get

全世界都知道	the whole world knows that
让开	move out of my way
让我猜一猜	let me guess
让我检查一下哨子	let me check my whistle
让我来	allow me
让我们保持联系	let's keep in touch
让我们好好庆祝一下吧	let's celebrate
让我们去拜访他们吧	let's go visit them
让我们往好处想吧	let's hope for the best
让我们言归于好吧	let's make up
让我们言归正传	let's get to the point
让我想想	let me see
让我想一想	let me see
让我这么说吧	let me put it this way
人多智广	two heads are better than one
人工的,人造的	artificial
人靠衣装	clothes make the man
认可	confirm
如果我是你,我就不会担心	I wouldn't worry about it, if I were you
如果我站在你的立场上	if I were in your shoes
入住登记	check-in

三思而后行	look before you leap
上楼	go up stairs
尚未决定	it's up in the air
烧酒	liqueur
少来这套	don't give me that
绍兴酒	shaohsing wine
伸展自己	stretching yourself
身份卡	ID card
时间差不多了	it's about time
时间就是金钱	time is money
时间快到了	time is up
使坚定	confirm
使用	use
世事难料	you never know
视情形而定	it all depends
是的,没错	yes, that's right
是时候了	it's about time
是这样	absolutely
数目看起来是对的	the figure seems all right
水壶	water jug
顺便说一句	by the way
说来话长	it's a long story

说时容易做时难	easier said than done
苏打水	soda water
算了吧	forget it
随你便	suit yourself
他并不在乎我	he doesn't care about me
他承认自己失败了	he owned himself defeated
他的样子总是滑稽可笑	his looks are always funny
他快步走路	he walks with a quick pace
他们按时取酬	they are paid by the hour
他们大大地表扬了他	they praised him highly
他身体已发育成熟	he is physically mature
他什么样的坏事都能干得出来	he is capable of any crime
他完成了这个任务	he has completed the task
他一点也不累	he was not a bit tired
他有不少的朋友	he has quite a few friends
他有惊人的记忆力	he has a remarkable memory
他有幽默感	he has a sense of humor
他正扮演一个老人	he is acting an old man
他正在找工作	he is looking for a job
它出故障了	it doesn't work
它很受欢迎	it's very popular

它绝对值得一看	it's worth seeing
它使我快要发疯了	it drives me crazy
她累垮了	she was totally exhausted
她心情不好	she's under the weather
太对不起了	I feel terrible about it
太离谱了	it's going too far
太遗憾了	what a pity
搪瓷杯	enamelled cup
陶瓷杯	ceramic cup
天呐	my god
天气渐渐凉爽起来	be growing cool
调酒杯	mixing glasses
调酒器	cocktail shaker
听到这个消息我感到遗憾	I'm sorry to hear that
听到这消息我很高兴	I'm glad to hear that
听起来很不错	it sounds great
退房	check-out
完全地	absolutely
玩得开心	have fun
晚饭我请客	dinner is on me
往左转/右转	turn left / right

威士忌	whisky
为安全起见	just to be on the safe side
为成功祈祷吧	keep your fingers crossed
为什么不	why not
我保证	I promise
我别无选择	I have no choice
我不干了	I quit
我不留神忘了	it slipped my mind
我不能抵挡诱惑	I can't resist the temptation
我不能肯定	I don't know for sure
我不确定	I'm not sure
我不是故意的	I didn't mean it
我不太清楚	I'm not really sure
我不习惯喝酒	I'm not used to drinking
我不知道	I've got no idea
我穿过了公园	I walked across the park
我到时随机应变	I'll just play it by ear
我的电话坏了	my phone was out of order
我的身体状况很好	I'm in good shape
我的压力很大	I'm under a lot of pressure
我得试试这么做	I'll have to try that

我独自一人,但并不觉得寂寞	I was alone, but not lonely
我对工作烦死了	I'm fed up with my work
我非常喜欢	I enjoyed it very much
我非常喜欢英语	I'm crazy bout English
我赶时间	I'm pressed for time
我感觉不舒服	I'm not feeling well
我给搞糊涂了	I'm lost
我过一会儿打给你吧	let me get back to you
我好久没见到你了	I haven't seen you for ages
我很抱歉	I apologize
我很受感动	I was moved
我很随和	I'm easy to please
我很想吃饺子	I feel like having some dumplings
我怀疑	I doubt it
我回来了	I'm home
我会安排一切的	I will arrange everything
我会回答你的	I'm going to answer you
我会记着的	I will never forget it
我会记住的	I'll keep that in mind
我会留意的	I'll keep my eyes open
我会想起来的	it will come to me

我会小心一些的	I will be more careful
我简直不敢相信	I can't believe it
我简直说不出话来	I could hardly speak
我见到了老板本人	I meet the boss himself
我将会尽我最大努力	I'll do my best
我将随兴而定	I'll play it by ear
我接受你的忠告	I'll take your advice
我今天心神不宁	I'm not myself today
我就是你的幸运舞伴啦	I'm your lucky fellow then
我就要这些	that's all I need
我拒绝	I decline
我看一看能怎么办	I'll see what I can do
我来办这件事	I'll take care of it
我来帮助你	I'll give you a hand
我来付帐	It's my treat
我马上就到	I'll be right there
我马上就来	I'll be right with you
我买不起	I can't afford it
我买不起一部新车	I can't afford a new car
我没有办法	I couldn't help it
我没有头绪	I have no idea
我没有意识到	I wasn't aware of that

我们边吃边谈吧	let's talk over dinner
我们的处境相同	we are in the same boat
我们都忙于工作	we are all busy with work
我们过得去	we can get by
我们今天就到这儿吧	let's call it a day
我们可以解决这个问题	we can work it out
我们去问一下吧	let's find out
我们是好朋友	we are good friends
我们有很多相同之处	we have a lot in common
我们走在花园小径上	we walk on the garden path
我迷路了	I'm lost
我明白了	I see
我盼望着这件事	I'm looking forward to it
我欠你晚餐的钱	I owe you for my dinner
我欠你一个人情	I owe you one
我亲眼所见	I saw it with my own eyes
我请客	my treat
我去查一下	I'll check it
我去接电话	I'll get it
我确信你能做到	I bet you can
我让你来点	I'll leave it to you
我认为你是不对的	I don't think you are right

我身无分文	I'm broke
我是他的球迷	I'm his fan
我手头正忙	I've got my hands full
我受不了	I can't stand it
我说不准	I can't tell
我说话算数	I mean what I say
我送你到门口	I'll walk you to the door
我随你	whatever you think is fine with me
我听见有人在笑	I heard some one laughing
我同意	I agree
我头痛	I've got a headache
我完全明白	I understand completely
我完全同意	I couldn't agree more
我为你感到非常骄傲	I'm very proud of you
我为人人,人人为我	all for one, one for all
我无能为力	there is nothing I can do
我希望你能原谅我	I hope you'll forgive me
我喜欢各种各样的水果	I like all kinds of fruit
我喜欢有你做伴	I enjoy your company
我现在确实很想去见他	I do want to see him now
我现在心情很好	I'm in a good mood
我羡慕你	I envy you

我想存点儿钱	I'd like to deposit some money
我想订票	I'd like to make a reservation
我想你常常跳舞吧	I suppose you dance much
我想请你吃晚饭	I'll treat you to diner
我想是这样	I suppose so
我想我得了感冒	I think I've caught a cold
我想要退款	I'd like a refund
我想预订一个房间	I want to reserve a room
我向你保证	I assure you
我要报一宗盗窃案	I want to report a theft
我要告诉你一个消息	I've got news for you
我要了	I'll take it
我要投诉	I have a complaint
我要一份和那个一样的	I'll have the same as that one
我也是	me too
	so am I
我也是这么想	that's just what I was thinking
	that's the way I look at it, too
我也一样	so do I
我也有同感	I feel the same way
我也这样以为	I thought so, too
我一点儿都不知道	I haven't the slightest idea

我已经吃饱了	I've had enough
我已经改变主意	I've changed my mind
我有权知道	I have the right to know
我有一个意想不到的东西给你看	I have a surprise for you
我又不是三岁小孩	I wasn't born yesterday
我在赶时间	I'm in a hurry
我在流口水了	my mouth is watering
我这就上路	I'm on my way
我真的非常后悔	I really regret it
我正在节食	I'm on a diet
我正在努力	I'm working on it
我正在找兼职工作	I'm looking for a part-time
我正准备打电话给你	I was just about to call you
我知道那种感觉	I know the feeling
我知道有关它的一切	I know all about it
我只会做那件事	I can do nothing but that
我只是随便看看	I'm just having a look
我指给你看	I'll show you
我终于找到你了	I get hold of you at last
我准备好了	I'm ready
我仔细考虑一下	I'll think it over

我自己冲洗照片	I develop films myself
我自己可以应付	I can manage
我总算想起来了	that rings a bell
我做到了	I just made it
我做这个很在行	I'm good at it
西柚	grapefruit
吸管	straw
习以为常了	that's always the case
下不为例	it won't happen again
先到先得	first come first served
相信你自己	believe yourself
相信我的话	take my word for it
香槟杯	champagne glass
香槟酒	champagne
香槟桶	champagne bucket
小冰桶	ice bucket
小费	tip
小孩伤心地抽泣着	the child sobbed sadly
小事	it's nothing
小心	be careful
小心不出大错	better safe than sorry
谢谢你的建议	thank you for your advice

谢谢你的提醒	thanks for the warning
心之所愿,无事不成	nothing is impossible to a willing heart
欣赏	enjoy
信不信由你	believe it or not
星星太遥远了	the stars are too far away
行李	luggage
行李及小费	luggage and tip
幸好知道了这件事	that's good to know
休想	forget it
削冰器	ice shaver
雪碧	sprite
洋葱	onion
要不要由你	take it or leave it
也许下一次吧	maybe some other time
也许这个办法会有效	maybe it will work
一点声音也没有	not a sound was heard
一定要小心	to be careful
一分钱一分货	you get what you pay for
一举两得	kill two birds with one stone
一切都准备好了	everything is ready
一切由你决定	it's up to you
一式三份	triplicate

一言为定	it's a deal
以同样的方式滚动	roll in the same way
易碎的	breakable
饮料	drink
英雄所见略同	great minds think alike
樱桃	cherry
用	use
用餐	having meals
由你决定	it's up to you
有了它真是方便	It really comes in handy
有你的电话	there is a call for you
有人在按门铃	someone is ringing the bell
有什么事吗	what's up
有时间我们聚一下吧	let's get together sometime
有一个会议	have a meeting
有用的	useful
有这个可能	there's a possibility
与你无关	none of your business
圆锥形酒杯	tapering glass
越快越好	as soon as possible
越快越好	the sooner, the better
再见	see you

再接再厉	keep up the good work
再试试	try again
再说吧	we'll see
再一次	again
在二(三)楼	on the second (third) floor
咱们别浪费时间了	let's don't waste our time
账单	bill
照我做的去做	do as I do
这边请	this way
这不关你的事儿	it's none of your business
这不是一个错误	it's not a fault
这才是上半场呢	this is only the first half
这对我来说无所谓	it doesn't matter to me
这个很时兴	it's up to date
这个汤非常美味	this soup tastes great
这很好	that's neat
这很容易	it's a piece of cake
这会对你有好处	it will do you good
这就是生活	that's life
这没什么大不了的	it's no big deal
这没有意义	it doesn't make sense
这世界真小	it's a small world

这事儿我得想一想再定	I'll have to see about that
这事可能发生在任何人身上	it can happen to anyone
这是必要的	it's essential
这是不可能的	it's out of the question
这是常有的事	these things happen all the time
这是个小问题	it's a pinch
这是浪费时间	it's a waste of time
这是你应得的	you deserve it
这是微不足道的	it isn't much
这是违法的	it's against the law
这是我的荣幸	it's my pleasure
这是一场友谊赛	it's a friendly competition
这是一生难得的机会	it's a once in a lifetime chance
这是最流行的款式	that's the latest fashion
这双鞋不太合适	these shoes don't fit right
这需要时间	it takes time
这样太耽误时间了	it really takes time
这真是苦不堪言	it's a pain in the neck
这正是我所需要的	it is just what I need
这正是我想要的	it's just what I had in mind
这只是时间问题	it's only a matter of time

真是好主意	that's a terrific idea
真是太巧了	what a coincidence
真是笑死我了	you're really killing me
真是一言难尽	it's a long story
真是遗憾	what a shame
真讨厌	that's disgusting
真糟糕	it's awful
振作起来	cheer up
正是如此	absolutely
知识就是力量	knowledge is power
只是为了消遣一下	just for entertainment
制冰机	ice maker
钟爱这项运动	love this game
注意	attention
	be careful
注意不要生病了	be careful not to fall ill
祝福你	bless you
祝好运	good luck
祝贺你	congratulation
祝你好运	good luck
祝你玩得开心	enjoy yourself
祝你下一次好运	better luck next time

祝您过得愉快	have a good time
自己的	own
自助餐	buffet
总比没有好	it's better than nothing
足球迷	a football fan
最简短的回答是干	the shortest answer is doing
左侧	the left side
做得好	good job
做个决定吧	make up your mind

附录2 "鹰眼挑战"常用语

本方发球时未踏线犯规	a non-tread foul on the service of the party
本方击球未触标杆	do not touch the stick of the ball
本方未过中线犯规	the party has not passed a foul in the middle line
本方未踏进攻线犯规	the party has not stepped into a foul
不管是不是你的球	whether it's your ball or not
裁判提名	referee nomination
第二裁判	the second referee
队员触网	the players touch the net
队员未触网	the players did not touch the net
对方触网	the other side of the net
对方发球时踏线犯规	a foul on the other side of the service
对方过中线犯规	a foul in the middle line
对方击球触标杆	the opponent hits the ball and touches the lever
对方踏进攻线犯规	each other stepped into a line of foul
对方未触网	the other side did not touch the net

发球踏线	serve tread
发球未踏线	serve no tread
过中线犯规	overline foul
击球踏线	hitting tread
击球未踏线	hitting no tread
快速攻击	quick attack
快速移动球	get to the ball with quick movement
面对目标区域	face the target area
请控制球	control the ball, please
球触标志杆	ball touches the marker
球触对方拦网队员	the ball touches the opponent
球触拦网队员	ball touches the blocker
球落本界外	the ball falls outside the boundary
球落对方界内	the ball landed in the other
球落界内	the ball landed in
球落界外	the ball fell out
球未触本方拦网队员	the ball did not touch the blocker
球未触标志杆	ball did not touch marker
球未触拦网队员	the ball did not touch the blocker
提出挑战	give a challenge
挑战成功	challenge success
挑战内容	challenge content

挑战失败	the challenge of failure
未过中线	not crossing the middle line
我的手在网下沿	my hands were below the top of net
我向某人发出警告	I give the warning to somebody
信号显示"触手出界"	signal displays "touch out"
在移动时观看球	watch the ball on moving

附录 3　记录常用语

安装	installation
备用球网	spare net
备用网柱	spare post
比分操控台	score control console
比赛被迫间断	the game is broken
比赛结果	match result
比赛名称	name of the competition
比赛球	game ball
编辑比赛数据	edit game data
标志杆和备用标志杆	marker and reserve marker
不符合规定的请求	improper request
擦地拖把	brush to mop
擦球毛巾	wipe the ball towel
场地面积	site area
得分	point
照度 1 500 勒克斯	light 1,500 lex
电视台	television station
电子记分表	electronic recording
	electronic scoreboard

	e-scoresheet
电子记分屏	electronic score screen
三十米钢尺	30 meters steel ruler
发球	service
发球次序	service order
发球得分	service point
发球轮次	service rounds
蜂鸣器	buzzer
该队阵容不完整	the X team is incomplete
各种提示曲	various hints
观众向场内抛洒物品	spectators threw something
广播台	radio station
国歌	the national anthem
国际记分单	international scoresheet
国家代码	country code
国旗(国际,参赛国)	national flag (international, participant country)
合法替换	legal substitutions
换人牌(1~20)	substitution cards (1 - 20)
换人时的比分	score at substitution
恢复时间	recovery time
记分表	scoresheet

记录表	scoresheet
剪刀	scissor
交换场区	change side
教练椅	coach chair
接发球	receive
结束时间	end time
界内外球	bound inside and outside the ball
警告	W
	warning
酒精检测仪(国际)	alcohol tester (international)
局间计时表	inter-set timing table
局间音乐	inter-set music
局结束	set over
局开始	set start
决定局	the deciding set
开始时间	strat time
开始新的比赛	start a new match
开始阵容	lime-up of strating player
可放12球轮车	a 12-ball wheel
(自由防守队员)控制表	Libero control sheet
快擦手毛巾	quick mopper towel
两支球队都是同样	both teams are similar

临时换衣间(国际)	temporary dressing room (international)
马扎	campstool
每局结束	end of each set
排队	line up
排球新规则	the new volleyball rules
判罚	P
	penalty
	sanction
判罚出场	E
	expulsion
判罚区	penalty area
气筒	the pump
气压表	the barometer
弃权比赛	match in default
球队位置表	team line-up
球架	the ball rack
球网丈量尺	the net measure ruler
取消比赛资格	disqualification
入场国旗(国际)	entrance flag (international)
3×3米准备活动区	3×3 meters to prepare the activity area

三分钟恢复时间	3-mins to recovery time
设备	equipment
胜队	winner
湿度计	moisture meter
手动计分显示板	manual scoring display board
首发阵容	starting line-up
司线旗	line of the flag
塑胶场地	plastic field
特殊替换	exceptional substitution
提出挑战	challenge
替补裁判	substitute referee
替补司线	second line
替补自由人背心	sub-free men's vest
替换	substitution
挑战次数	number of challenges
挑战结果	challenge result
挑战界面	challenge interface
挑战内容	challenge content
挑战手势	challenge gesture
透明胶带	lucency tape
网上麦克风(国际)	online microphone (international)
网上摄像机(国际)	online video camera (international)

网柱	the post
网柱套	sheath of post
位置表	line-up sheet
温度计	thermometer
系统需求	system requirement
下载比赛	load match
线绳	cord
小型手动记牌	small hand card
新比赛	new match
选择侧面和服务	choose the side and service
摇把	crank
1×1米判罚区	1×1 meter penalty area
衣物车	clothing car
医务人员	the medical staff
因标志杆断裂造成的间断	the broken antenna for the interuption
因电视转播要求造成的延误	TV request for the delay
因器材问题造成的延误	equipment problems delaying the start
因球网破损或脱落造成的间断	the torn or dawn net for the interuption

因上一场比赛时间的拖延造成的延误	prolongation for the previous match
因停电造成的间断	electric power failure for the interuption
鹰眼系统	challenge system
运动队(国际)	sports team (international)
运动员席	substitution bench
在比赛前	before the match
在比赛中	during the match
暂停计时表	pause the chronometer
阵容不完整	team is incomplete
主办者	the organizer
自由人记录表	Libero control sheet
自由人受伤	the injured Libero
自由人替换表	Libero control sheet

附录4　裁判员常用语

通知开会

蒂芙妮：(电话中)喂，我是蒂芙妮。您是王先生吗？

王：是的，我是。

蒂芙妮：早上好，睡得好吗？

王：很好，谢谢！

蒂芙妮：9点钟我们有个会议。那么，你可以现在用早餐吗？我们已在餐厅了。

王：没问题，我准备好了。可是你能告诉我开什么会吗？

Call for meeting

Tiffany: Hello, this is Tiffany. Is that you, Mr. Wang?

Wang: Yes (this is), speaking.

Tiffany: Good morning, did you sleep well?

Wang: Yes I did, thank you!

Tiffany: We are going to have a meeting at 9 o'clock. So, should you have your breakfast now? We are here at the restaurant.

Wang: All right, I'm ready. But, would you tell me what's the meeting about?

蒂芙妮:不太清楚,不过我想可能要会见仲裁和特别裁判委员会吧。	Tiffany: I'm not sure, I think we'll meet the Jury and SRC there.
王:很好,谢谢!	Wang: That's good, thank you!
蒂芙妮:一会儿见。	Tiffany: See you later.
王:一会儿见。	Wang: See you later.

裁判员实习 **Practical clinic**

蒂芙妮:喂,王,下午好。	Tiffany: Hello, Wang, good afternoon.
王:下午好,蒂芙妮,我们去哪儿?	Wang: Good afternoon, Tiffany, where are we going?
蒂芙妮:去体育中心。我们在那儿实习。您带着裁判服了吗?	Tiffany: We are going to the Sports Center. We'll practice there. Have you carried your uniform?
王:带了。	Wang: Yes, I have.

蒂芙妮:您可能是第二局的第一裁判。	Tiffany: You may be the first referee in the second set.
王:真的?我看看带哨子没有。噢,带着了。	Wang: Really? Let me check my whistle. Yes, it's here.
蒂芙妮:另外,请您告诉我您的上衣和鞋子的号码。	Tiffany: By the way, please tell me the size of your shirt and shoes.
王:上衣是 X0 号,鞋子是 27 号。	Wang: My shirt is X0 and my shoes is 27.
蒂芙妮:好了,谢谢!	Tiffany: OK, thank you!

裁判任命书 / Referee nomination

裁判任命书	REFEREE'S NOMINATION
王先生(中国):	Mr. Wang (CHN):
您被任命担任以下比赛裁判工作:	You are nominated to officiate the following match:
波兰 对 意大利	POL vs ITA
性别　　　女队	SEX　　　F

男队	M
担任第一裁判员	In the position of 1st. referee
城市:罗马	City:Rome
体育馆:巴拉兹托	Hall:Palazzeto
日期:2016.5.10	Date:10/5/2016
时间:20:30	Time:20:30
特别裁判委员会	Special Referee Commission
主 席	Chairman
(签 名)	Sign

会见裁判员　　　　　　　**Meeting the referees**

王:您好,蒂芙妮。您是第二裁判吗?

Wang:Hi, Tiffany. Are you the second referee?

蒂芙妮:是的。

Tiffany:Yes, I'm.

王:噢,和你一起工作,太高兴了。

Wang:Oh, so glad to work with you.

蒂芙妮:我也是。

Tiffany:So am I.

王:让我见一见其他裁判员好吗?

Wang:May I meet other referees?

蒂芙妮:当然。他是史密斯,记录员。他是汉森,司线员……

王:很高兴认识你们。

蒂芙妮:你不跟我们说些什么吗?

王:没什么。只有一点,如果你们确实看清楚了,请给我打触拦网手出界的手势。就这些,你还有什么吗,蒂芙妮?

蒂芙妮:没有。

王:好,预祝顺利。

蒂芙妮:祝顺利。

Tiffany: Of course. He's Smith, the scorer. He's Hunson, the line's man ...

Wang: Glad to meet you.

Tiffany: Don't you speak something to us?

Wang: Nothing. But just one point, please signal the "touch out by the block" only if you have seen it with absolute clarity. That's all, have you anything else, Tiffany?

Tiffany: Nothing.

Wang: OK, good luck.

Tiffany: Good luck.

检查场地器材

王:嗨,蒂芙妮!

Check the court and equipment

Wang: Hi, Tiffany!

蒂芙妮:什么?	Tiffany: Yes?
王:丈量尺在哪儿? 我看网子可能有点高。	Wang: Where's the measuring rod? I think the net is a bit higher.
蒂芙妮:也许在记录台下面吧。对,是在这儿,还有比赛球。	Tiffany: Maybe, it's under the scorer's table. Yes, it is and including the game balls.
王:你看这球怎么样? 是不是气太足了?	Wang: What do you think about the ball? It's too hard, isn't it?
蒂芙妮:是太足了,不过其余的还可以。	Tiffany: Yes, it is, but the others are OK.
王:这回行了。你检查过号码牌了吗?	Wang: That's all right. Have you checked the number cards?
蒂芙妮:检查过了,很齐全。	Tiffany: Yes, I have, it's complete.
王:让我们试试凳子上的蜂鸣器吧!	Wang: Let's see the buzzers on the bench!

蒂芙妮:我来吧,你最好去试一试裁判台。	Tiffany: I'll do that, you'd better try the referee's stand.
王:没问题。	Wang: It's OK.
蒂芙妮:好,一切就绪。	Tiffany: Yes, everything is ready.

挑边 — **Toss the coin**

裁判员:你是队长吗?	Referee: Are you the captain?
A:我是。	Captain A: Yes, I am.
裁判员:可是你胸前没有标记。	R: But there's not mark on your chest.
A:是,我马上弄上。	A: Yes, I will put it on immediately.
裁判员:让我们挑边吧。你猜哪一面?	R: Let's toss the coin. Which side do you guess?
A:我猜"字"。	A: Word.
裁判员:你猜对了。你要什么?发球?好,你先发球。你呢?你要哪一边?	R: Yes, it is. What do you want? Service? OK, service first. Then which side do you want?

B：我要左边吧。	Captain B：The left side.
裁判员：你们要一起做准备活动呢，还是分开？	R：Do you want to make your warm-up together or separately?
A：分着吧！	A：Separately!
裁判员：好吧，一共6分钟。你们先练，告诉她们把首饰都摘下来。	R：OK, six minutes in all. You take first, and tell them to take off their jewelry.

场上位置   **Game position**

第二裁判员：先生，位置表？	Second referee：Line-up sheet, sir?
教练：给您。	Coach：Here you are.
第二裁判员：请签上名字。	2nd R：Sign please.
教练：噢，对不起。	Coach：Oh, I'm sorry.
第二裁判员：谢谢。你们的位置错了。	2nd R：Thank you. Your position is wrong.
教练：哪儿？	Coach：Where?

第二裁判员:一号位应该是8号,可你们是7号。 2nd R: The right back should be No.8, but you have No.7.

教练:噢,天哪! 我可以改一改吗? Coach: Oh, dear! May I change it?

第二裁判员:不行! 位置表不能更改。 2nd R: No! The sheet can't be changed.

教练:可是8号队员没有来呀。 Coach: But No.8 is not here.

第二裁判员:如果你坚持让7号上场,你必须请求换人。 2nd R: If you want to keep No.7 on, you must request for substitution.

教练:那好,我换人。 Coach: That's all right, I'll do.

第二裁判员:可以。意大利队请求换人。7号上,8号下。好了吗? 2nd R: OK. Substitution of Italy team. No.7 in, No.8 out. Ready?

回答问题

队员：不！不！我没犯规。我的手低于球网上沿。

裁判：队长！

队长：是，先生。可是怎么回事？我们不懂为什么犯规？

裁判：好，我来回答你，4 号是后排队员。他触球低于球网上沿，所以他不是拦网犯规，但那是第一次击球。在此之后，你们又击球三次，所以你们是四次击球犯规。

队长：噢，明白了，先生。对不起！

Answer questions

Player: No! No! It's not a foul. My hands were below the top of net.

Referee: Captain!

Captain: Yes, sir. But what's the matter? We don't understand why you whistled for foul?

R: Yes, I am going to answer you, No. 4 is back line player. He contacted the ball below the top of the net, so it wasn't blocking foul, but it was the first contact. After that, you hit the ball three times, so you had four hits.

C: Oh, I see. I'm sorry!

裁判:还有,4号队员不许跟我说话。现在我给予他警告。

R: And No.4 cannot speak to me. Now, I give the warning to him.

队长:是,先生。

C: Yes, sir.

发球次序错误

记录员:裁判!

二裁:什么事?

记录员:A队发球次序错误。

二裁:确实吗?应该是谁发球?

记录员:7号!

二裁:让我看看。是的。7号,你应该在1号位。对了,她们在犯规时得了多少分?

记录员:两分。

Fault in rotation

Scorer: Referee!

2nd R: What happened?

S: Team A was fault in rotation.

2nd R: Are you sure? Who should serve?

S: No.7!

2nd R: Let me see. Yes, it is. No.7, you should be right back. Right, and how many points were scored during the foul?

S: Two points.

二裁:那么取消 A 队所得 2 分,换发球。记好了吗?	2nd R: So, cancel two points of Team A, then change service. Are you ready?
记录员:记好了。	S: I'm ready.
二裁:继续比赛!	2nd R: Resume the play!

附录5 教练员常用语

致词

女士们、先生们：
谢谢你们对我的热烈欢迎和精心安排。

我非常高兴能担任冰岛HK俱乐部的教练员。

我也希望能成为冰岛人民的好朋友。

在我任职期间,我将竭尽全力做好工作。

我相信我能与其他教练员以及运动员们很好合作的。

谢谢大家!

Speech

Ladies and Gentlemen:
Thank you very much for your warm welcome and nice arrangements for me.

I'm very happy to be a coach of HK club in Iceland.

And also I hope to be a good friend of Icelander.

During the period of my staying here, I'll do my best to work well.

I'm sure I can cooperate well with the players and other coaches.

Thank you!

了解情况

吴：王教练,我听说你过去是 HK 的教练,对吗?

王：是的,我也一直是个队员。

吴：哦,那太好了。你能给我提供一些关于球队的情况吗?你知道这对我的工作是很重要的。

王：当然可以。你想知道什么呢?

吴：你们俱乐部里有几支排球队?

To understand the situation

Wu: Hello, coach Wang, I heard that you were the coach of HK club, weren't you?

Wang: Yes, I was and I have been a player too.

Wu: Oh, that's good. Could you give me some information about the teams? You know it's important for my work.

Wang: Certainly. What do you want to know?

Wu: How many teams in your club?

王:五支队。有两支男队,两支女队将由你训练。另外的一支队是老头队,我是队长,希望你能和我们一起来练习。

Wang: There are five teams. Two boys and two girls, they will be trained by you. The other one is an old boy team, I'm the captain and I hope you will play with us.

吴:那太好了。不过我在我们国家队做队员还是很多年前的事了,我好久没打球了。

Wu: Oh, that would be wonderful. But I used to be a player of our national team many years ago, I haven't played for a long time.

王:那没关系。你会发现他们是很有趣的家伙,这帮老头。

Wang: It doesn't matter. You'll find that they are very interesting fellows, those old boys.

吴:肯定是的,不过那些年轻队员们呢?

Wu: Sure, but what about the boys and girls?

王：啊，男一队是个很好的队，去年是冰岛甲级队的第3名。女一队第5名。另外的两个队是青年队，我们寄希望于你呢！

Wang: Yes, the first team of boy is a very good team, it placed on No.3 of the first class teams in Iceland last year. And the first team of girl was No.5. The two other teams are junior teams, we place hopes on you!

吴：谢谢，我尽力而为。让我们共同努力吧！

Wu: Thank you, I'll do my best. Let's fight together!

谈计划

各位好，我来此地已经两个星期了。

今天我想谈一谈训练计划的问题。

你们都是很好的运动员，素质好，斗志高，训练刻苦。

Talk about the plan

Hello every one, I've already been here for two weeks.

Today, I want to talk something about the training plan.

You are very good players, good fitness, high spirit of fighting, and training hard.

| 但是如果你们想要有较大的飞跃,你们就需要花费更多的精力去提高你们的技术,你们的技术太粗糙。 | But if you want to make a big progress, you should spend more energies to heighten your technical skills, for yours are too rough. |

所以,在圣诞节之前,训练的主要内容是你们的技术动作规范,而且要训练如何在比赛中去运用它们。 | So before Christmas, the main program of training is to standardize your technical movement, and practice how to use it in the game.

圣诞节之后,我想该是大赛的决赛阶段了。 | After Christmas, it's the final stage of the big tournament, I think.

那时,我们要注重战术训练。 | We should pay attention to tactics.

但是前一部分是后一部分的基础 | But the first part is the basis of the second part.

没有技术就没有战术。 | Without technique, there will be no tactics.

另外,训练的时间太短了。 | By the way, the training time is too short.

至少,每次训练我们需要 2 小时以上。	At least, we need more than two hours each time.
能办到吗,王教练?	Can you make it, coach Wang?
(王:我试试吧。)	(Wang: I'll try it.)
好,就谈这些,谢谢。	OK, that's all, thank you.

准备活动 / Warm-up

教练员:你们好,今天谁缺席?	Coach: Hello, who is absent, today?
队员:埃纳尔正在换衣服。	Player: Einer is changing.
教练员:好,训练之前,让我们做些准备活动。	Coach: Good, before practice let's do some exercises for warm-up.
首先绕场地慢跑。	First jogging around the court.
听到我的哨声双手触地。	Touch the floor with two hands on hearing the whistle.
然后继续跑。	Go on then.

交叉步跑。	Run with side cross step.
好,停!	OK, stop!
下一练习仰卧撑30次。	Next, push-up 30 times.
仰卧起坐30次。	Sit up 30 times.
鱼跃,从这儿到那边的端线再回来!	Dive, from here to the end line over there and return!
嘿,加油!跟紧一点!	Hi, come on! Follow closely!
滚翻,同样做又一个来回!	Roll in the same way!
自己拉一拉肌肉,韧带。	Stretching yourself.
现在做熟悉性的练习,两人一组!	Now ball handling drills with partners!
两人一组打防练习……	Pepper drill with partners ...

训练——技术 Ⅰ

教练员：今天我来告诉你们垫球的标准基本姿势。

看,两脚分开与肩同宽。

重心放在双脚前脚掌的内侧,脚跟抬起。

两膝和髋屈曲接近90度,膝关节在脚趾之前,肩关节在膝关节之前,重心前倾。

两手置于体前自然伸出相当于腰的高度。

Practice — technique Ⅰ

Coach: Today, I'll show you what's the fundamental stance for digging.

Look, the feet are spread apart as the shoulder width.

And the center gravity of the body is on the inside balls of the feet, the beets off the floor.

The knees and hip are bent nearly 90°, knees in front of the toes, shoulders in front of the knees, the body weight leans forward.

The hands are extended frontally about waist high.

好,跟着我做!	Well, do as I do!
很好,保持微动,注视球,以快速的移移去找球。	Good, watch the ball on moving, get to the ball with quick movement.
面对球垫出的方向。	Face the target area.
两臂伸直,肘夹紧,用小臂触球。	Look the elbows, straight arms and contact the ball on the forearms.
不要挥臂击球。	Don't swing the arms at ball.
对,这次对了。	Yes, that's right.
现在来接球。	Now, receive the balls.
注意!	Attention!
移动! 低姿!	Move! Get low!
动! 不要只是伸手去够球,要选位对正球。	Go! Don't just only reach the ball, to get in fight position facing the ball.

再来!	Again!
……	…

训练——技术 Ⅱ   **Practice — technique Ⅱ**

教练员:分两组扣球,快攻手扣近快在三号位,强攻手在四号位扣平拉开。

Coach: Two groups spike, the quick hitters spike quick-A from area three, power hitters spike shoot-sets from area four.

嗨,看着一传,注意上步节奏!

Hi, watch the first pass, pay attention to the rhythm of approach.

怎么回事,卡尔?

What's the matter, Karl?

作为一名快攻手,你必须跑每一个球!不论它是好球,还是坏球。下一个练习是扣调整球,轮流做二传。

To be a quick hitter, you must run for every ball! No matter it's good or not. Next, spike deep-sets, and be setter in turn.

用力跳！要注意脚跟到脚掌的过渡。	Hard jump! Pay attention to the heel-to-toe transition.
埃纳尔，用手掌和手指向上裹住球，用甩腕动作使球上旋。	Einer, wrap your palm and fingers up and over the ball, producing a top spin with wrist snap.
对,这个好！	OK, that's good!
嘿,太棒了！	Hi, wonderful!
现在,扣直线,注意起跳点。	Now, spike deep straight line, pay attention to the take-off point.
卡尔,不要乱扣！请你控制球！	Karl, don't shoot at random! Control the ball, please!
埃纳尔,放松一点！	Einer, relax!

训练——战术 I Practice — tactic I

教练员：今天我们要练习交叉、假交叉和梯次进攻。　　Coach: Today we are going to practice cross, fake cross and tandem tactics.

三个人网前进攻,三个人在后排接我的球,三个人在对面拦网。	Now three boys stand close to the net, three receive my balls on the back court, and three block on the opposite side.
盖里,二传。其余的人给我供球。	Gerry, the setter. The others supply balls for me.
首先,三号位跑近体快球,二号位跑交叉,四号位跑平拉开。	First, the middle run the quick-A, the right run the cross and the left run for the shoot-set.
不对!不对!你跑得太晚了。	No! No! You are too late.
他来不及扣这个球,因为他只能在你之后起动,你明白吗?	He can't catch and spike the ball because he has to start after you, understand?
对了,这回对了。	Yes, that's right.
盖里,平拉开应该再拉开点!	Gerry, the shoot-set should be wider!

嗨,别偷懒。每个球都要认真跑,不论是不是你的球。	Hi, don't be lazy. Every one must run truly, whether it's your ball or not.
彼此交换位置!	OK, change position!
下面,二号位跑假交叉,其余不变。	Next, the right one runs for the fake cross, the others are the same.
现在中间的不变,二号位跑背溜,四号位跑梯次。	Now the middle is the same, the right runs for quick D and the left runs for the tandem.
最后,你们可以通过暗号联系打其中的任何一种。可是拦网队员得好好注意判断他们了。	Last, you may play anyone of those with your secret signal. But the blockers have to read them well.
咱们来一个比赛吧,看你们哪一方先得 10 分获胜。	Let's have competition and watch who will win ten points first.

训练——战术 Ⅱ

教练员: 现在我们来训练如何防对方四号位的拉开进攻。

盖里,你在一号位防直线。

可是如果直线被二号位队员封住了,你要注意跟进保护吊球。

五、六号位注意防斜线,而且做好向前移动的准备。

但是如果盖里跟进五、六号位要注意直线的底角。

Practice — tactic Ⅱ

Coach: Now we practice how to defend a wide set with middle back defense.

Gerry, you are in area one and defend the straight line.

But if it's covered by the end blocker you should run in to cover the dink shot.

Middle-back and left-back, you should defend cross court and be ready to move forward.

But the middle-back should take care of tine corner of straight line as Gerry has run in.

四号位,你是不拦网的队员,你该干什么呢?	Left-front, you are off-blocker, what will you do?
对,你应当迅速撤下以便防守对方的小斜线扣球。	Yes, you should back off the net quickly in order to dig the sharp crosscourt spike.
这样,三个后排队员和一个前排队员就构成了马蹄形的防守圈,并且相互保护策应。	So, the three back-row players and left-front constitute a half-moon formation and support each other.

身体训练	Conditioning exercise
轮换练习 Ⅰ	Circle drill program Ⅰ (on the court)
日期:十月十二日	Date:12th Oct
时间:35分钟	Time:35 mins
重复次数:3	Repetition:3
内容:慢跑与疾跑交替进行 4 次	Activities:jog and sprint alternately for 4 times
全力跳 4×10 次	4×10 maximum jumps

鱼跃 10 次　　　　　10 dives
两侧交替滚翻　　　10 rolls to alternate side
各 10 次
俯卧撑 50 次　　　　50 sit ups
(慢跑包括雀跃、侧滑　(jogging includes with
步跑、交叉步跑、后退　skipping, side steps,
跑和跑跳步。)　　　cross-steps, running
　　　　　　　　　　backward and hopping.)

轮换练习 Ⅱ　　　　**Circle drill program Ⅱ**
(负重练习)　　　　**(weight training)**
内容　组次重复次数　Activities Sets-Repetitions
　　　(重量)　　　　　　(Weight)
深蹲　3×25(15,10)　Squats 3×25(15, 10)
(重量要与练习内容和　(The weight should be heavy
组次相适应,这样规定　enough for each set, so that
的重复次数才能完成。)　the prescribed number of
　　　　　　　　　　repetitions can properly
　　　　　　　　　　be done.)

提踵　3×10　　　　　Toe raises 3×10
小腿屈伸　3×10　　　Leg extensions　3×10
卧推　3×10　　　　　Bench press　3×10

实力推(硬推) 3×10	Military press 3×10
拉力 3×10	Pulleys(Lat pull downs) 3×10
双杠推起 3×12	Parallel bar dips 3×12
引体向上 3×尽可能	Chin-ups (palms facing 3×as many as possible)
俯卧撑 3×30	Push-ups 3×30
蹲跳 3×30	Squat jumps 3×30
12分钟跑	12 minutes run
准备活动后,首先做深蹲练习,其他各组练习要衔接紧密。各项练习完成之后返回第一项做第二组练习。	The squats should be done first after warm-up, the other exercises should be done in sequence. Then go back and do the second set of all of them.
如果想采用间歇训练法,可以不做12分钟慢跑。	If you are taking interval training, then forget the twelve minutes run.

准备会

教练员:今天我们要和IS队打比赛。他们是去年第2名。你们怎么看这场球?

Preparatory meeting

Coach: Today we are going to play with IS team. They were the second place last year. What do you think about this match?

A: 我看我们能赢。

B: 我们当然能赢,我们比去年有很大进步。

教练员: 好,可是我们的优点是什么,他们的缺点是什么呢?

C: 快攻!我们的快球比他们快,而且,我看他们在比赛中运用也不行。

B: 我们的防守比他们好。

教练员: 还有呢?

A: 他们的一传不好,而且他们情绪不稳定。

A: I think we can win over them.

B: Yes, we are certain to be victorious, we have had more progress than last year.

Coach: Yes, but what's our strong points and what's their weak points?

C: Quick attack! Our quick ball is faster than theirs, and I don't think they play it well in the game.

B: Our defense is better than theirs.

Coach: And then?

A: Their digpass is not good, and their emotion is not stable.

教练员：对,但是你们只谈了一个方面,另一个方面如何呢?	Coach: Yes, but you have just talked one side, what's the other side?
B：他们比我们高、拦网好、扣球力量大。	B: They are taller than us, they block well and spike hard.
教练员：好,那咱们的弱点呢?	Coach: Good, what's our weakness?
C：急躁。	C: Impetuous.
B：连续失误。	B: Lose continually.
教练员：好,你们说的很对。所以今天第一件事就是一传。它是快攻的保证。我们必须以快攻突破他们的拦网。所以一定要保持冷静,注意垫好一传。	Coach: Yes, you are quite right. So, today, the first thing is about digpass. It's the guarantee of quick attack. We have to play quick to break their block. Keep calm to make great efforts to digpass.

| 第二件事是拦网。是的,他们比咱们高大、有力,但是他们扣球的路线很简单。 | The second is block. Yes, they are high and strong, but their spike course is very simple. |

只要拦住斜线就可以了。两个人都拦斜线,晚一点儿起跳。

Just block their crosscourt is OK. Two blockers cover the crosscourt and jump a bit later.

另外……

And the others ...

好,最后我要说,当然,我们会胜的。但首先要努力完成以上各项!

OK, the last word is that, surely we will win but fight for the accomplishment of the all!

换人

教练员:卡里,过来!你准备替换7号,等他转到后排时换!

Substitution

Coach: Kally, come here! You are going to change No.7 when he turns to back-row!

上去后跳发球，破坏他们的一传，然后防对方9号的大力扣杀。	Take the jump service to break their receiving, then dig the hard spike of No.9.
准备好了吗？	Are you ready?
上场！	Go on!
裁判员，换人。7号下！10号上！	Referee, substitute. No.7 out! No.10 in!

暂停   **Time out**

教练员：怎么回事，小伙子们？	Coach: What's the matter, boys?
我们连失3分全是因为一传。	We have lost three points because of digpass.
埃纳尔，别光想进攻，首先要接一传。	Einer, don't just think about attack, digpass is first.
卡尔，别紧张，要相信自己！	Carl, don't be nervous, believe yourself!

盖瑞,一传不好不要打快攻,给埃纳尔传高球,他扣球时大家保护他。	Gery! Don't play the quick if the digpass is not good, pass the high-set to Einer, and all of you cover him when he spikes.
还有拦9号。别跟球,他只是一条斜线。	Then block the No.9. Don't follow the ball, he has just one course that's crosscourt.
记住!	Remember it!
加油!现在是关键时刻!拼!	Come on boys! It's a pinch! Fight!

参 考 文 献

[1] 李建亚,周密.体育基础英语[M].北京:化学工业出版社,2015.

[2] 刘振忠,荣晶.体育通识英语1[M].北京:清华大学出版社,2016.

[3] 董进霞.通向北京奥运:多国会话ABC[M].北京:北京体育大学出版社,2005.

[4] 田华实,杨方.用英语说中国:体育[M].上海:上海科学普及出版社,2009.

[5] 卜存英.奥林匹克词汇大全:英汉对照分项图解[M].南京:河海大学出版社,1988.

[6] 中国排球协会.气排球竞赛规则[M].北京:北京体育大学出版社,2016.

[7] 中国排球协会.排球竞赛规则(2013—2016)[M].北京:人民体育出版社,2013.

[8] 中国排球协会.排球竞赛规则(2017—2020)[M].北京:人民体育出版社,2017.

[9] SILVA M, LACERDA D, JOAO P V. Game-related volleyball skills that influence victory[J].

Journal of human kinetics, 2014, 41 (1): 173-179.

[10] ZAHRADNIK D, UCHYTIL J, FARANA R, et al. Ground reaction force and valgus knee loading during landing after a block in female volleyball players [J]. Journal of human kinetics, 2014, 40(1): 67-75.

[11] MERGHES P E, GRADINARU S. Comparative Analysis of the "Libero" in great Performance Volleyball[J]. Timisoara Physical Education and Rehabilitation Journal, 2014, 6 (12): 23-28.

[12] GRADINARU S, MERGHES P E. Considerations on the constitutional type of the central hitter in volleyball[J]. Timisoara Physical Education and Rehabilitation Journal, 2014, 7 (13): 27.

[13] CIESLA E, DUTKIEWICZ R, MGLOSIEK M, et al. Sports injuries in Plus League volleyball players [J]. The Journal of sports medicine and physical fitness, 2015, 55: 628-638.

[14] BOLACH B, STANDO M, BOLACH E. Training load in direct start preparation (DSP) in sitting volleyball players[J]. Physiotherapy, 2015, 23(4): 14-23.

[15] HUDSON C, GARRISON J C, POLLARD K. Y-balance normative data for female collegiate volleyball players [J]. Physical Therapy in Sport, 2016, 22: 61-65.

[16] SIMONA T D, MIRCEA N, FLORIN T. The Progress of the Volleyball Game by Efficiency of Ⅱ—line Attack[J]. Procedia-Social and Behavioral Sciences, 2015, 180: 1374-1379.

[17] BOROZAN I S, GRADINARU S, MIRON P, et al. Postural differences of volleyball players [J]. Timisoara Physical Education and Rehabilitation Journal, 2016, 9(17): 42-46.

[18] SACCOL M F, ALMEIDA G P L, DE SOUZA V L. Anatomical glenohumeral internal rotation deficit and symmetric rotational strength in male and female young beach volleyball players [J]. Journal of Electromyography and Kinesiology, 2016, 29: 121-125.

[19] GJINOVCI B, IDRIZOVIC K, ULJEVIC O, et al. Plyometric Training Improves Sprinting, Jumping and Throwing Capacities of High Level Female Volleyball Players Better Than Skill-Based Conditioning[J]. Journal of sports science & medicine, 2017, 16(4): 527.

[20] CZAPLICKI A, SLIWA M, SZYSZKA P, et al. Biomechanical Assessment of Strength and Jumping Ability in Male Volleyball Players During the Annual Training Macrocycle[J]. Polish Journal of Sport and Tourism, 2017, 24(4): 221-227.

[21] COSTA G C, CASTRO H O, EVANGELISTA B F, et al. Predicting Factors of Zone 4 Attack in Volleyball[J]. Perceptual and motor skills, 2017, 124(3): 621-633.

[22] ZAHRADNIK D, JANDACKA D, HOLCAPEK M, et al. Blocking landing techniques in volleyball and the possible association with anterior cruciate ligament injury [J]. Journal of sports sciences, 2018, 36(8): 955-961.

[23] BISAGNO E, MORRA S. How do we learn to "kill" in volleyball?: The role of working memory capacity and expertise in volleyball motor learning[J]. Journal of experimental child psychology, 2018, 167: 128-145.